At Home Café

GREAT FOOD AND FUN FOR EVERYONE

Helen Puckett DeFrance & Leslie Andrews Carpenter

WITH CAROL PUCKETT

RODALE

To the kids who inspired us:
Rob, William, Myers, Annie, Martin. and Katie

Illustrations by Dea Dea Baker

Photographs © Mitch Mandel / Rodale Images

Book design by Christina Gaugler

Library of Congress Cataloging-in-Publication Data

DeFrance, Helen Puckett.

  At home cafe : great food and fun for everyone / by Helen Puckett DeFrance and Leslie Andrews Carpenter.

      p.   cm.

  Includes index.

  ISBN-13 978-1-59486-842-9 hardcover

  ISBN-10 1-59486-842-5 hardcover

  1. Entertaining. 2. Cookery. 3. Menus. I. Carpenter, Leslie Andrews. II. Title.

TX731.D448 2008

642'.4—dc22   2007050679

Distributed to the trade by Macmillan

2 4 6 8 10 9 7 5 3 1 hardcover

RODALE

LIVE YOUR WHOLE LIFE™

We inspire and enable people to improve their lives and the world around them

For more of our products visit **rodalestore.com** or call 800-848-4735

Contents

Introduction

*A*t *Home Café* springs from the heartfelt enthusiasm of two women with an important message to share. Helen Puckett DeFrance and Leslie Andrews Carpenter created *At Home Café* out of devotion, tenacity, and a desire to spread the gospel of families cooking together. These recipes have been tested both in their own family kitchens and by the thousands of students whom these gifted teachers have taught to cook in hundreds of classes.

My younger sister, Helen Puckett DeFrance, is the fourth of six children in our big, noisy family from Jackson, Mississippi. She learned to cook at the apron strings of our beloved grandmother, Helen Todd. She also inherited our mother Dorothy Puckett's flair for entertaining and hospitality. She helped plan her own 5th birthday party, at which she and her friends made and decorated cupcakes. She always headed up the annual holiday cookie baking for the neighbors and our father's office Christmas party. Helen grew up to own a catering-and-takeout business, pursued a master's degree in education, and created a successful career in cooking classes for families.

Leslie Andrews Carpenter grew up in the Mississippi River town of Greenville, where entertaining was—and still is—an art form practiced with an intensity bordering on religious fervor. The cooks of this area are serious about their biscuits, pie crusts, and cheese straws, and their recipes aren't passed around lightly. Leslie was raised in a family of four children, and the center of family life was the kitchen table, over which Leslie's mom, Mary Lynn Andrews, graciously presided. The Andrews' kitchen was a popular gathering place for friends and guests because the cookie jar was never empty and the refrigerator was magically filled with tasty dishes, ready to be delivered to a friend or neighbor at a moment's notice. Children were welcome helpers in the Andrews' kitchen, and Leslie developed a love of cooking at her mother's side. She parlayed a degree in education and the skills she learned in the family kitchen into a real-world career as a caterer and cooking teacher.

When Leslie and Helen teamed up to teach cooking classes at my store, the Everyday Gourmet, they developed a rapport fueled by their shared beliefs that home cooking is important to modern family life. At a time when paper sacks of food are handed through a drive-thru window and the back-seat of a minivan has replaced the family table, these two women are passionate advocates for cooking and eating as a family. They believe that cooking is an invaluable life tool often overlooked in our fast-paced world. They are united by their belief in the importance of the "family table" as the emotional center of the home.

Everywhere they taught, their message of cooking together as families resonated with audiences. Before long, folders of recipes, piles of notes, and legal pads full of ideas and recipe starts were unceremoniously dumped on my kitchen table. "What should we do?" Helen and Leslie asked. My answer was, "I think you have a book somewhere in all of this."

The guiding principle for the book was that it should be family-friendly and easy to use—a cook-book that a parent would pick up instead of calling for takeout. Chapters are organized by menus ranging from school-night suppers to backyard parties, and the collection of themed menus is inspired by Leslie and Helen's experiences as mothers and home cooks. The menus promote healthy, balanced, nutritious fare, simple enough for everyday family meals and sophisticated enough for an elegant dinner party. Each menu comes with tips on how to simplify the cooking process and advice on what can be prepared ahead. Individual shopping lists for each chapter are conveniently tucked in a pocket at the back of the book.

The menus are conducive to whole-family participation, advocating a hands-on approach that involves the entire family in every aspect of meal preparation—grocery shopping, cooking, eating the delicious results, and cleaning up. In the back of the book are safety tips and other notes for kids, detailing basic cooking techniques with clear and easy-to-understand instructions. The recipes are simple enough for children to master but delicious enough for their parents to serve at a dinner party.

With the publication of *At Home Café,* these extraordinary women are taking their message of bringing families together through cooking into homes all across America. Leslie and Helen present us this marvelous collection of experience-tested recipes that are fun to create, delicious to eat, and always liberally seasoned with enthusiasm, patience, and love. We hope you will share their experience in your own kitchen.

Carol Puckett
President of the Viking Hospitality Group, Viking Range Corporation, Greenwood, Mississippi
Founder of the Everyday Gourmet, Jackson, Mississippi

Acknowledgments

Our deepest appreciation goes to our families: mothers and fathers, brothers and sisters, nieces and nephews, sisters-in-law, cousins, and most of all our children for their continued love and support in this project.

We thank Bess Reed Currence, who believed in us enough to make our elusive dream a reality and who, through much patience and hand holding, helped us to create this book; and Michael Psaltis for his wisdom in guiding us on this project as well as his willingness to understand our "Southern language." Our great appreciation also goes to Liz Perl, who took an impromptu meeting with us, immediately saw the importance of our message, and made the leap to publish it; and to our editor Shea Zukowski, without whose patience and skill under such a tight deadline this book would not have happened.

We are eternally grateful to the entire team at the Everyday Gourmet in Jackson, Mississippi, for allowing us the opportunity to build our kids' classes at their legendary cooking school, and to Fred and Margaret Carl and the lively crew at Viking Range Corporation in Greenwood, Mississippi, who invited us to take our show on the road. Joe Sherman, Bob Pavy, Kathleen Bruno, and the talented cooks at the Viking Cooking School took on the daunting task of recipe testing and magically made it happen, and for that we're most grateful. We thank the incomparable Martha Stewart for introducing us to a national audience by inviting us to appear on the *MARTHA* show.

We'll be forever baking cookies to thank our friends and neighbors who tested, tasted, and served as sounding boards. Tom MacDonald, Chris Gaugler, Marc Sirinsky, Joan Parkin, Pam Simpson and Colleen Kobrick are tops on our list for their attention to every detail during our cover shoot.

Carol Puckett, sister, friend, and mentor, helped us convert our dream into print, showed us the steps we needed to take, and lovingly guided us through each one.

Heartfelt thanks to Kreis Beall, who was one of the first to believe in our vision and who helped make it possible by inviting Helen to create the kids' cooking program at the renowned Blackberry Farm, and Sam Beall for his continued support and belief in the program.

Most of all, we thank all of the children, past and present, who have honored us by allowing us to teach them to cook.

Saturday Morning Breakfast

Homemade Buttermilk Biscuits

Sausage Pinwheels

Sweetest Sweet Rolls

Fluffy Pancakes

Kettle Tea

Saturday morning breakfast is a magical family time when we break the hurried weekday routine, and the kitchen takes on a more leisurely and relaxed atmosphere. Some of my fondest childhood memories are of Saturday mornings with my father, brothers, and sister crowded into the tiny horseshoe-shaped kitchen on Bellewood Road.

There were six kids in the family, and with our wide range of ages and myriad activities, there was a lot of coming and going during schooldays. Saturday was and still is "together time." My father, who typically left for work in the early morning and returned after bedtime, was our weekend playmate and breakfast cook. It was Mom's time off, and we enthusiastically pitched in and helped Dad in the kitchen. Pancakes were a special treat, with Dad or the oldest children entrusted with flipping them. Our family repertoire also included homemade buttermilk biscuits, sweet rolls, and omelets with country sausage. With so many helping hands in such a small space, we could turn out a quantity of food that would rival a short-order café.

Fresh-squeezed orange juice has also become a staple in my own home with my son, Martin. Making orange juice to accompany a menu like this was one of the first activities he learned in Montessori school at the age of 2. I cut the oranges in half, and he could squeeze them himself. His favorite cooking request was "Help me do it myself!" I also shared with Martin the tradition of Kettle Tea, a breakfast beverage I learned about from my grandfather. Children love being included in menu planning and cooking and really do like to eat most of the things we eat as adults. Kettle Tea is their "coffee."

Leslie remembers family birthday breakfasts where she was encouraged to "eat her age" in pancakes and assures me that she really did eat 16 pancakes on her 16th birthday!

Homemade Buttermilk Biscuits

4 cups all-purpose flour

1½ teaspoons baking powder

½ teaspoon baking soda

1 teaspoon salt

1 cup shortening or butter

2 cups buttermilk

Preheat oven to 450°.

Place flour, baking powder, baking soda, and salt in a mixing bowl and mix thoroughly with a whisk or fork. Cut in shortening or butter until mixture resembles coarse crumbs.

Add buttermilk. Stir just until dough sticks together.

Form dough into a ball, and fold over and over on a lightly floured surface.

Pat out dough to ½-inch thickness.

Cut with a biscuit cutter.

Place on an ungreased baking sheet, close together for soft-sided biscuits or 1 inch apart for crisp-sided ones.

Bake for 5 minutes.

Reduce oven to 400° and bake for 8–10 minutes more.

Yield: about 20 biscuits

Kitchen Notes

- For tender, flaky biscuits, pat out the dough instead of rolling it.
- For easy cleanup, work with the dough on lightly floured parchment paper, waxed paper, or a silicone baking mat.
- To make your own buttermilk, use 1 tablespoon of whole milk, add 1 tablespoon of vinegar, and let it sit for a couple of minutes.

Sausage Pinwheels

1 recipe Homemade Buttermilk Biscuits (opposite page)

1 16-ounce roll sausage (mild or hot)

Preheat oven to 400°.

Prepare Homemade Buttermilk Biscuit dough as directed and place on a piece of lightly floured waxed paper.

Pat dough into a 14- by 10-inch rectangle about ¼ inch thick.

Crumble uncooked sausage evenly over dough.

Beginning at the long side, roll up jelly-roll style, using waxed paper to help make it into a long roll.

If not used immediately, the roll may be wrapped in foil and frozen for 1 month or refrigerated overnight.

Slice roll into ½-inch pinwheels.

Place on a baking sheet, almost touching, and bake for about 15–18 minutes, or until brown.

Enjoy!

Yield: about 2 dozen

Kitchen Notes

- To prevent overworking, gently pat out the dough with your hands instead of using a rolling pin.
- To keep dough from sticking while patting out, flour the work surface and your hands.

Sweetest Sweet Rolls

SWEET ROLLS:

1 cup whole milk

6 tablespoons sugar

1 package active dry yeast

3 cups plus 2 tablespoons all-purpose flour, plus more for rolling out dough

½ teaspoon salt

6 tablespoons unsalted butter, softened

1 egg

1 teaspoon vegetable oil

CRUNCHY FILLING:

¾ cup packed light brown sugar

1 cup crushed cornflakes

2 tablespoons plus 2 teaspoons ground cinnamon

½ teaspoon salt

12 tablespoons unsalted butter, melted

GLAZE:

2½ cups confectioners' sugar

4 tablespoons half and half

1 teaspoon vanilla extract

TO MAKE SWEET ROLLS:

Heat milk in a small saucepan over medium-low heat until warm. Remove from the heat.

In a small mixing bowl, combine 2 tablespoons sugar with yeast and whisk in warm milk, and let rest until slightly thickened and foamy, about 5 minutes.

Sift flour, salt, and remaining 4 tablespoons sugar into a large mixing bowl. Add butter, egg, and yeast mixture. Stir well with a large wooden spoon until all flour is mixed in.

Place dough on a work surface sprinkled with 3 tablespoons flour and knead until smooth and elastic, about 3–5 minutes. If dough is sticky, add a bit more flour and continue kneading to work it into the dough. (Alternatively, mix dough in an electric mixer fitted with a dough hook.)

Using your hands, form dough into a ball and lightly grease it with oil.

Place dough into a large mixing bowl and cover with plastic wrap. Let rest in a warm, draft-free place and allow to rise about 1½ hours to double.

When dough has risen, divide it into 2 equal portions.

(continued)

TO MAKE CRUNCHY FILLING:

In a small mixing bowl, combine filling ingredients, stirring until smooth.

TO ASSEMBLE SWEET ROLLS:

Place one portion of dough on a lightly floured surface. Rub a rolling pin with flour and roll dough into a large rectangle, about 12 inches by 9 inches.

Using a spoon, sprinkle half of filling over top of dough.

With the long end of the rectangle facing you, roll up dough, jelly-roll style.

Pinch edges together and use a serrated knife to cut 1½-inch-thick slices.

Place rounds on a large baking sheet, allowing room in between each roll for the final rise.

Repeat with remaining dough.

Cover rolls with plastic wrap and let rest in a warm, draft-free place until risen by half their original size and almost touching, about 1 hour.

Make sure the oven rack is in the center position, and preheat oven to 350°.

Bake until golden brown, about 30 minutes.

TO MAKE GLAZE:

Combine glaze ingredients in a medium mixing bowl and stir until smooth.

Remove sweet rolls from oven and drizzle glaze over tops.

Serve warm.

Yield: 18 large or 24 medium rolls

Kitchen Notes

- To crush cornflakes, place them in a sealed plastic storage bag and crush with your hands or a rolling pin.
- When using yeast, always check the expiration date. If the yeast doesn't bubble, start over with new yeast.
- To prevent sticking, coat your rolling pin with flour before rolling out the dough.
- The best way to roll dough evenly is in a pattern: north, south, east, and west.
- Paintbrushes are not just for art class but also for food. Kids always enjoy painting the sweet rolls before the rolls go in the oven.

Fluffy Pancakes

2 cups milk

4 tablespoons butter, melted

2 eggs, beaten

2 cups all-purpose flour

½ teaspoon salt

1 teaspoon baking powder

2 teaspoons sugar

In a large bowl, mix milk, butter, and eggs.

In a separate bowl, sift flour, salt, baking powder, and sugar.

Add sifted dry ingredients to the milk, butter, and egg mixture. Whisk just until mixed.

Ladle ¼ cup batter on a hot, lightly buttered griddle or skillet.

Cook on medium-high heat until bubbles form all over top of pancake.

With a spatula, turn and cook on other side.

Enjoy!

Yield: 16–18 pancakes; 6 servings

Kettle Tea

1 cup milk

2–3 teaspoons sugar, to taste

½ teaspoon vanilla extract

Heat milk in a microwave-safe coffee mug for 1 minute on high in the microwave.

Add desired amount of sugar and vanilla extract.

Stir lovingly.

Yield: 1 serving

Kitchen Notes

- When making tea on the stove top, use low heat and be careful not to scald the milk.
- Heat only slightly when serving to kids.

Get Up & Go!
Breakfast

"Bomber" Biscuits

On-the-Go-A.M. Breakfast Sandwich

Wacky Waffles

Made-with-Love Blueberry Muffins

Fruitini

The sound of someone yelling "Get up and go!" resonates through my childhood memories and recalls frenetic mornings of trying to get to school on time. Admittedly, "get up and go" is a phrase I overuse with my own four children as we hurriedly dress, eat breakfast, collect books, and finish the last little bit of the previous night's homework before the horn honks for the car pool.

In my childhood family, breakfast was the one meal of the day that we ate as a family. It was my father's fervent wish that we start the day together, and so we did just that. Hair may have been in rollers, and sometimes the car pool would have to wait—the Andrews family was at the breakfast table!

Since the entire family was in attendance, the breakfast table was the natural setting for jokes, pranks, and tricks of all kinds. One April 1, my brothers and sister and I blissfully sat in our pajamas at the breakfast table when a horn started honking, announcing the car pool's arrival. We scrambled to our rooms, threw on clothes, and rushed outside, only to find our father standing in the yard yelling "April fool!" It's a practical-joke tradition I've enjoyed with my own children. One April morning a few years ago, I woke my four children, admonishing them to get up and go because Mr. Herring, the school principal, was downstairs for breakfast. They were panicked, mortified, and then, of course, furious at their mom when there was no Mr. Herring. They were even more furious the next year, when Mr. Herring actually appeared. He went from bed to bed waking each child while I smugly stood behind him, saying "April fool!"

With a big family, there is never a dull moment at the breakfast table. We are big breakfast eaters, and in my way of thinking, it's the most important meal of the day for my husband and children. I set the table at night to give myself a little extra time in the morning and use seasonal paper products to brighten the meal and give the family a little surprise.

"Bomber" Biscuits

8 ounces sour cream

1 cup club soda

4½ cups biscuit mix

¼ cup butter, melted

Preheat oven to 450°.

Combine sour cream with ½ cup club soda in a large bowl.

Add 4 cups biscuit mix and stir with a wooden spoon until blended. Add remaining ½ cup club soda. Mix only until blended.

On a lightly floured surface, gently pat out dough to about a 1-inch thickness.

Use remaining ½ cup biscuit mix as needed to keep dough from sticking.

Cut with a large biscuit cutter. Place on a baking sheet and brush with melted butter. Bake for 15 minutes.

"Bomber" Biscuits taste just like Popeye's biscuits!

Yield: 8 large biscuits

Kitchen Notes

- Handle the dough as little as possible and you will have tender, light biscuits.
- To make ahead, cut out biscuits, place on a baking sheet, and freeze the entire sheet.
- Once frozen, place in a plastic storage bag and retrieve as needed. Baking sheet can go from freezer to oven.

On-the-Go-A.M. Breakfast Sandwich

1 recipe "Bomber" Biscuits (opposite page) or 1 10.2-ounce can refrigerated buttermilk biscuits

6 eggs

1 teaspoon salt

½ teaspoon black pepper

3 tablespoons milk

1 tablespoon butter

¾ cup (about 4 ounces) chopped cooked ham or bacon

½ cup Cheddar cheese

If using canned biscuits, bake according to the package directions.

Meanwhile, in a medium bowl, combine eggs, salt, pepper, and milk. Using a wire whisk, beat until foamy.

Melt butter in a medium skillet over medium heat. Add ham or bacon and sauté for 2 minutes.

Reduce heat to low and pour egg mixture into skillet. Cook 4–6 minutes, or until egg mixture is set, stirring and turning occasionally. Stir in cheese.

Slice open biscuits and spoon egg mixture onto bottom halves. Cover with top halves.

Enjoy.

Yield: 8 servings

Kitchen Notes

- Customize filling using your choice of ham or bacon and a favorite cheese.
- This is a high-protein "brain booster" breakfast.

Wacky Waffles

3 eggs

1 cup club soda

½ cup buttermilk

1 teaspoon baking soda

1¾ cups all-purpose flour

2 teaspoons baking powder

½ teaspoon salt

½ cup vegetable oil

Preheat a waffle iron. Coat with nonstick cooking spray.

In a mixing bowl, combine all ingredients and stir with a whisk until blended.

Pour into a small pitcher or measuring cup.

Pour batter into waffle iron and cook until crisp and golden.

Yield: 8 servings

Kitchen Notes

- Club soda makes for a light and crisp waffle.
- The surface of the waffle iron becomes very hot. Be careful not to touch.
- Batter may be stored in the refrigerator for 2 days.

Made-with-Love Blueberry Muffins

⅔ cup shortening

1 cup sugar

3 eggs

3 cups all-purpose flour

2½ teaspoons baking powder

1 teaspoon salt

1 cup milk

2 cups blueberries

Preheat oven to 375°.

Grease muffin tins or line with muffin cup liners.

Cream shortening and sugar until fluffy.

Whisk eggs together in a bowl and add to mixture.

In a separate bowl, sift flour, baking powder, and salt.

Alternately add flour mixture and milk to creamed ingredients, beginning and ending with flour mixture.

Gently fold in blueberries.

Pour into muffin tins, filling each cup ¾ full.

Bake for 15 minutes if using mini-muffin pans, 35–40 minutes if using a regular-size muffin pan.

Yield: 16–18 regular-size muffins

NOTE: This batter will keep in the refrigerator for up to 1 week. Store in an airtight container and use as needed for fresh, hot muffins.

Kitchen Note

- For easy cleanup and less mess, use paper muffin liners—great for weekday mornings before school.

Fruitini

8 cups of your favorite fresh fruit—
cantaloupe, kiwifruit, strawberries,
bananas, grapes, oranges

8 stemmed glass

Juice of 2 lemons

Confectioners' sugar

Make balls out of melon. Slice kiwi, strawberries, bananas, and grapes. Section oranges. Mix together in a bowl.

Dip rims of glasses into a shallow bowl of lemon juice.

Put confectioners' sugar in another bowl and dip rims in confectioners' sugar.

Fill glasses with fresh fruit.

Top with a sprinkle of confectioners' sugar.

Serve.

Yield: 8 servings

Kitchen Notes

- To ensure best flavor, use seasonal fruits.
- To extract maximum juice from the lemon, cut it in half and heat in the microwave for 20 seconds on high before juicing.

Lazy Morning Brunch

Overnight Oven-Baked French Toast

Crispy Brown-Sugar Bacon

Cheddar Cheese Grits Casserole

Absolutely Delicious Danish

Lazy Morning Muffins

azy mornings are a welcome and delicious reprieve from the hectic pace of our everyday lives. Guaranteed to coax even the grumpiest sleepyhead out of bed, our lazy morning menu also dresses up nicely for a Christmas brunch or any other special occasion. Whenever my mom has out-of-town guests, she calls on me to cook this brunch. In my role as family caterer, I have cheerfully explained the intricacies of preparing a Southern breakfast to many an inquisitive guest around her table. "What exactly *is* a grit?" they ask, or "Why do you put sugar on bacon?" (Because it tastes so good.)

My mother's well-set table and gracious style of entertaining define Southern hospitality for me and for the guests she entertains from around the corner or across the country. I have learned from her that the warmth of hospitality is just as important as the food that is served. The table is always inviting and set with colorful linens and china, and, as hostess, she is prepared, relaxed, happy, and eager to spend time with her guests.

This menu is simply Southern, easy to execute, and always delicious. When *Southern Living* magazine published a story on Leslie and me, this is the menu they chose. The French toast is assembled the night before so it can be popped into the oven the next morning. Grits are a traditional Southern favorite, but every transplanted Southerner who has served these far away from home has won new converts. When my son Martin and I found ourselves "gritless" in Southern California, my family sent them by Federal Express. Absolutely Delicious Danish is a specialty of Leslie's sister, Kim, who never goes to a family gathering without them, and Lazy Morning Muffins were a signature dish during my years as a caterer in Dallas. The batter can be kept in the refrigerator and used as needed.

Overnight Oven-Baked French Toast

¼ cup butter

12 ¾-inch-thick slices French bread

6 eggs, beaten

1½ cups milk

¼ cup sugar

2 tablespoons maple syrup

1 teaspoon vanilla extract

½ teaspoon salt

Confectioners' sugar

Grease a 9- by 13-inch ovenproof glass pan. Lightly butter one side of bread. Place buttered bread in pan, butter side up.

Mix eggs, milk, sugar, syrup, vanilla extract, and salt in a bowl and pour mixture over bread, turning slices to coat. (Butter side will be down now.)

Cover with foil and refrigerate overnight.

Preheat oven to 400°.

Remove foil from pan. Bake until golden brown, about 40–45 minutes. After 20 minutes, turn bread to bake evenly.

Sprinkle with confectioners' sugar and serve.

Yield: 6 servings

Kitchen Note

- The perfect make-ahead breakfast dish: Dip your bread, place in the casserole dish, cover with foil, and refrigerate overnight. Pull out and bake while the coffee is brewing.

Crispy Brown-Sugar Bacon

1 pound regular sliced bacon, at room temperature

1 cup light brown sugar, firmly packed

1 tablespoon cracked black pepper (optional)

Preheat oven to 425°.

Line a sheet pan with aluminum foil.

Cut each slice of bacon in half.

Mix brown sugar and pepper, if using, in a shallow bowl.

Thoroughly coat each slice of bacon with brown sugar mixture.

Twist and place on sheet pan.

Bake for 20–25 minutes, or until crisp.

Cool on foil.

Serve at room temperature.

Yield: 6–8 servings

Kitchen Notes

- We like to place a wire rack on a sheet pan and put the bacon on the rack. This allows the bacon to drain and makes it nice and crispy.
- Leftover bacon is great crumbled on top of a salad or used in a BLT.

Cheddar Cheese Grits Casserole

1 quart milk

¼ cup butter

1 cup uncooked grits

1 teaspoon salt

½ teaspoon ground black pepper

1 egg

2 cups (8 ounces) shredded Cheddar cheese

½ cup (2 ounces) grated Parmesan cheese

Preheat oven to 350°.

Grease a 2-quart casserole dish.

Slowly bring milk to a boil over medium heat. Add butter and stir until melted.

Add grits. Cook, stirring constantly, about 5–7 minutes, or until mixture is the consistency of oatmeal.

Remove from heat.

Add salt, pepper, and egg. Whisk until well combined.

Stir in Cheddar with a wooden spoon.

Pour into casserole dish.

Sprinkle with Parmesan. Bake for 35–40 minutes.

Yield: 6 servings

Kitchen Note

- If you're on the go, buy cheese already grated at your local market.

Absolutely Delicious Danish

2 8-ounce cans crescent dinner rolls

16 ounces cream cheese, softened

1½ cups sugar

1 egg

1 teaspoon vanilla extract

1 teaspoon almond extract

5 tablespoons butter, melted

¾ teaspoon ground cinnamon

⅔ cup chopped almonds

Preheat oven to 350°.

Grease a 9- by 13-inch baking dish.

Unroll 1 can of rolls and press into bottom of dish, pressing perforations together to form flat sheet of dough.

Press edges of dough slightly up sides of dish.

Put cream cheese, 1 cup sugar, egg, and extracts in a mixing bowl.

Beat until smooth.

Pour into pan and spread over dough.

Open remaining can of rolls and place over cream cheese mixture, pinching perforations together. Press edges together to seal.

Combine butter, cinnamon, almonds, and remaining ½ cup sugar.

Spread evenly over top layer of dough.

Bake for about 30 minutes, or until golden.

Cool for at least 20 minutes before cutting.

To serve, cut into triangles or rectangles.

Yield: 8–12 servings

Kitchen Notes

- These are a snap to make and store in the freezer for unexpected guests.
- A universal favorite, they are also ideal when it's your turn to take treats to a meeting, school, or office function.

Lazy Morning Muffins (opposite) and Absolutely Delicious Danish (page 21)

Lazy Morning Muffins

4½ cups all-purpose flour

2½ cups sugar

2 tablespoons cinnamon

1 teaspoon salt

4 teaspoons baking soda

6 eggs

2¼ cups vegetable oil or canola oil

2 tablespoons vanilla extract

1 cup coconut

½ cup nuts (optional)

1 cup raisins

2 cups mashed fruit (bananas, peaches, strawberries, apples)

Preheat oven to 350°.

Line a muffin pan with muffin liners or grease the pan.

Sift together flour, sugar, cinnamon, salt, and baking soda. Set aside.

In a large bowl, mix eggs, oil, and vanilla extract.

Add sifted ingredients. Mix well.

Blend in coconut, nuts (if using), and raisins.

Fold in fruit.

Fill muffin cups ¾ full.

Bake for 15–18 minutes.

Yield: 3 dozen

Kitchen Note

- A bowl, whisk, and wooden spoon are perfect and simple tools to prepare these extraordinary breakfast treats.

Make-and-Take Picnic Lunch!

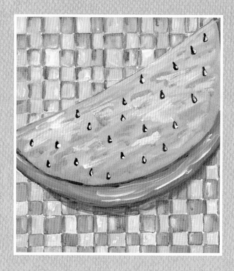

Buffalo Chicken Wraps with Yummy Blue Cheese Dressing

Gouda Pimiento Cheese Wraps

Chinese Chicken Wraps

Greek Wraps

Of Course, Peanut Butter and Jelly Wraps

"Ice Chest" Strawberry Soup

Raw Veggies with Spicy Comeback Sauce

Mud 'n' Worms

Watermelon Cookies

Picnics celebrate good weather and good times and enhance our sense of fun and adventure. Leslie and I both grew up in the Deep South, where picnicking is practically a year-round pleasure.

A picnic can be as simple as throwing a quilt on the ground in the front yard, stopping at a roadside park, or tailgating during football season. As a child, my favorite picnic was the Sunday family ritual at our summer home on the Mississippi Gulf Coast. We looked forward to summer Sundays, when Mother would place two patchwork quilts on the lawn under the ancient oak trees. There was always a pitcher of lemonade or iced tea on the wrought-iron table, and the picnic lunch could be as simple as a grocery bag full of po'boy sandwiches from a neighborhood eatery or as bountiful as a summer feast of fried chicken, fresh vegetables, and cold watermelon for dessert. The mood was always festive and lively, with children running in the yard, swinging under the arm of the giant oak, or playing a game of croquet.

As both a mother and a teacher of cooking, I am always promoting the art of picnicking. In fact, the theme of the first kids' cooking class I taught at Blackberry Farm, a resort in the foothills of the Smoky Mountains, was a Make-and-Take Picnic Lunch. It's been so popular that I've done it every year since. The kids and I spend the morning making each recipe on the menu, and then we hike to the boathouse, eat our picnic lunch, and canoe on scenic Walland Pond. Each summer as I prepare for Camp Blackberry, I think about how I could change up this class, but then I always realize that it's perfect just like it is. No matter how many times the children return for Camp Blackberry, they always want to make Mud 'n' Worms. Watermelon cookies are a hit with "kids" of all ages. They are so good that Sam Beall, the son of the proprietor of Blackberry Farm, asked if we could make them at Christmas as well!

Buffalo Chicken Wraps with Yummy Blue Cheese Dressing (opposite), Greek Wraps (page 30), and Raw Veggies with Spicy Comeback Sauce (page 32)

Buffalo Chicken Wraps with Yummy Blue Cheese Dressing

DRESSING:

½ cup sour cream

¼ cup mayonnaise

½ cup crumbled blue cheese

1 teaspoon cider vinegar

1 teaspoon fresh lemon juice

Dash of Tabasco sauce

½ teaspoon finely minced onion

½ teaspoon garlic, finely chopped

Salt and black pepper, to taste

WRAPS:

6 boneless, skinless chicken breast halves

2 tablespoons butter, melted

4 teaspoons Tabasco sauce

1 teaspoon Creole seasoning

6 tablespoons olive oil

1 teaspoon salt

1 teaspoon black pepper

¼ teaspoon cayenne pepper

½ cup orange juice

1 tablespoon Dijon mustard

1 teaspoon sugar

1½ cups shredded celery

1½ cups shredded carrots

2 cups diced cucumber, drained on paper towels

12 soft flour tortillas

TO MAKE DRESSING:

Combine sour cream and mayonnaise in a bowl.

Fold in blue cheese, then remaining ingredients.

This will keep for 3 days in the refrigerator.

TO MAKE WRAPS:

Rinse chicken and pat dry. Place in a large bowl.

In a small bowl, mix butter, Tabasco, Creole seasoning, and 2 tablespoons oil.

Pour over chicken and coat evenly. Marinate, covered, at room temperature for 30 minutes.

Heat grill to high.

(continued)

Combine salt, peppers, orange juice, mustard, sugar, and remaining 4 tablespoons oil.

Place chicken on grill and baste with juice mixture. Cook, turning once, about 4–5 minutes per side, or until nicely charred on the outside, and a thermometer inserted in the thickest portion registers 160°F and the juices run clear (may take longer for larger breasts).

Remove chicken from grill. Cool until able to touch, then slice into strips.

Put chicken, celery, carrots, and cucumbers in a bowl and toss with Yummy Blue Cheese Dressing.

Place 1 tortilla on a work surface and spread ½ cup mixture down the center.

Roll into a tight cylinder. Repeat with remaining tortillas and chicken mixture and serve.

Yield: 12 wraps

Gouda Pimiento Cheese Wraps

2 pounds Gouda or smoked Gouda cheese, shredded

2 3-ounce jars pimientos, drained and diced

1¼ cups mayonnaise

1 small white onion, grated (save juice)

1 teaspoon black pepper

10–12 soft tortillas

Put all ingredients, except tortillas, in a mixing bowl.

Mix thoroughly by folding with a spatula.

Spread mixture on tortillas and roll up.

Leftover Gouda Pimiento Cheese may be stored in a covered container for up to 1 week.

Yield: 10-12 wraps

Chinese Chicken Wraps

FILLING AND WRAPS:

1 6-ounce package slivered almonds

¼ cup sesame seeds

1 package ramen noodles, crushed

2 tablespoons butter

6 cooked skinless chicken breasts, shredded

½ head iceberg lettuce, shredded

4 green onions, chopped

¼ cup chopped cilantro

10–12 soft flour tortillas

DRESSING:

2 tablespoons sesame oil

¼ cup rice vinegar

¼ cup soy sauce

1 teaspoon salt

½ teaspoon black pepper

1 teaspoon sugar

1 tablespoon garlic chili sauce

TO MAKE FILLING:

Sauté almonds, sesame seeds, and noodles in butter until brown, about 4–5 minutes.

Place sautéed ingredients, chicken, lettuce, onions, and cilantro in a large bowl.

TO MAKE DRESSING:

Place all dressing ingredients into another bowl and whisk.

TO ASSEMBLE WRAPS:

Pour dressing over filling ingredients and toss until thoroughly combined.

Place 1 tortilla on a work surface and spread ½ cup filling down the center.

Roll up into a tight cylinder. Repeat with remaining tortillas and filling and serve.

Yield: 10–12 wraps

Greek Wraps

½ cup plain yogurt

2 tablespoons lemon juice

1 tablespoon white wine vinegar

½ teaspoon dried oregano

½ teaspoon salt

½ garlic clove, chopped

½ teaspoon black pepper

½ teaspoon Greek seasoning

FILLING:

6 chicken breasts, cooked

2 cups romaine lettuce, torn

1 cup diced tomatoes

½ cup diced cucumber

½ cup crumbled feta cheese

¼ cup sliced ripe olives

¼ cup chopped purple onion

10–12 soft flour tortillas

TO MAKE DRESSING:

Put all dressing ingredients in a bowl and whisk. Set aside.

TO MAKE FILLING:

Chop chicken and put in bowl with lettuce, tomatoes, cucumber, cheese, olives, and onion. Toss with reserved dressing.

TO ASSEMBLE WRAPS:

Place 1 tortilla on a work surface and spread ½ cup filling down the center.

Roll up into a tight cylinder. Repeat with remaining tortillas and filling and serve.

Yield: 10–12 wraps

Kitchen Notes

- These wraps can be either completed ahead of time or taken with you and assembled on the spot.
- When making wraps ahead, roll and seal them tightly in plastic wrap. They can be refrigerated for a day.
- Wraps can be served chilled, warm, or at room temperature.
- Use any style or flavor of tortilla—white, wheat, or even chipotle pepper, tomato, or spinach.

Of Course, Peanut Butter and Jelly Wraps

½ cup dried fruit bits (raisins or Craisins)

½ cup peanut butter

⅛ teaspoon cinnamon

6 soft flour tortillas

¼ cup your favorite jelly

In a small bowl, combine fruit bits, peanut butter, and cinnamon and mix well.

Spread mixture evenly over tortillas. Dot with jelly. Roll up.

Yield: 6 wraps

"Ice Chest" Strawberry Soup

5 cups strawberries, washed, sliced, and hulled

½ cup sugar or more to taste, depending on sweetness of strawberries

1 cup half and half

1 teaspoon almond extract

1 cup sour cream

Put all ingredients in a blender. Puree until blended.

Chill until ready to use.

Put in thermos and take on picnic.

Pour into small bowls and enjoy.

Yield: 6–8 servings

Kitchen Notes

- We recommend fresh strawberries, but unsweetened frozen strawberries will work just as well.
- Sip soup as a beverage or serve with a spoon.

Raw Veggies
with Spicy Comeback Sauce

SAUCE

3 cloves garlic, peeled

1 medium onion, chopped

½ cup ketchup

½ cup chili sauce

½ cup vegetable or canola oil

2 tablespoons water

2 tablespoons fresh lemon juice

1 tablespoon paprika

1 tablespoon Worcestershire sauce

1½ teaspoons Creole seasoning

1 teaspoon dry mustard

1 cup mayonnaise

VEGETABLES

Carrots

Celery

English cucumbers

Black olives, whole

Cherry tomatoes, whole

TO MAKE SAUCE:

Place all ingredients in the blender and pulse until blended.

Store in the refrigerator for up to 2 weeks.

TO MAKE VEGETABLES:

Cut carrots, celery, and cucumbers into strips about 3½ inches long and ¼ inch wide.

Pack in separate containers for your picnic.

Yield: 3 cups

Kitchen Notes

- You may have extra dip. It will last in the refrigerator up to 14 days. It is great on salads and as a spread for sandwiches as well.

- Use this scrumptious dipping sauce as a salad dressing or sandwich spread.

Mud 'n' Worms

MUD CUPS:

¼ cup butter

½ cup sugar

¼ teaspoon vanilla extract

1 large egg

1 cup all-purpose flour

3 tablespoons cocoa powder

⅛ teaspoon salt

FILLING:

1 package instant chocolate pudding mix (4-serving size)

½ cup sour cream

1 cup cold milk

½ cup chocolate cookie crumbs

24 gummy worms

TO MAKE MUD CUPS:

Cream butter and sugar until light and fluffy.

Mix in vanilla extract and egg until well combined.

Stir in flour, cocoa, and salt until dough forms a soft ball.

Cover dough and refrigerate for 30 minutes.

Divide into 24 portions. Roll into balls.

Press individual balls into bottoms and up sides of greased mini-muffin cups.

Bake at 350° for 8–10 minutes, or until firm and set.

Remove from oven and lightly press centers down using a small spoon. Cool.

Run point of sharp knife around top edges. Remove from pans.

TO MAKE FILLING:

Beat pudding powder, sour cream, and milk together in a medium bowl for about 1 minute, or until smooth.

Spoon into mud cups enough to fill to top of crust.

Sprinkle about 1 teaspoon cookie crumbs over each mud cup.

Insert worm partway into filling.

Yield: 24 cups

Watermelon Cookies

3½ cups all-purpose flour, sifted

1½ teaspoons baking powder

1 teaspoon salt

1 cup butter

1½ cups sugar

1 tablespoon vanilla extract

2 eggs

Red food coloring

1 package mini chocolate chips

2 cups confectioners' sugar

¼ cup water

Green food coloring

Preheat oven to 375°.

Line a baking sheet with parchment paper.

Sift flour.

Sift flour again with baking powder and salt and set aside.

Cream butter, sugar, and vanilla extract.

Add eggs and beat for 1 minute, or until fluffy. Slowly add dry ingredients until blended.

Add a few drops of red food coloring to dough. Continue to add a drop at a time until dough looks the color of watermelon.

Cover with plastic wrap placed directly on dough. Refrigerate for at least 30 minutes, or overnight. (Dough can be made ahead at this point and frozen.)

Roll out dough to ¼-inch thickness. Cut cookies out with a round cookie cutter, then cut each one in half. (You may find it easier to cut in half on the baking sheet.)

Place on baking sheet.

Place a few of the chocolate chips on each slice to make "seeds."

Bake for about 8 minutes.

TO MAKE ICING:

Put confectioners' sugar and water in bowl and mix with green food coloring, adding a drop at a time until the color of the outside of a watermelon.

You may need to add a little more confectioners' sugar or water to get the preferred consistency.

After cookies have cooled, roll round edges in green icing. This makes each one look like a slice of watermelon.

Yield: 6–7 dozen cookies

It's a School Night! Supper

Cheesy Meat Loaf

Carrot French Fries

Creamed Corn

Dynamite Orange-Almond Salad

Parmesan Cheese Biscuits

Hooray! For Hershey Bar Pie

The relentless dash from school to soccer practice to piano lessons is no excuse for fast-food school-night suppers. The supper table should be a place where the details of the day are shared and parents ask the universal question, "How was your day today?" We are both tired, busy moms with active children and frenetic lives, but one of our deepest beliefs is that many of the problems of modern life could be solved by spending time together at the family table. It doesn't matter whether you've got a small family of two or a big, noisy group like we both grew up in—the important thing is to share mealtimes together.

We think cooking should be a worthy after-school family activity as important as the sports and lessons in which our children participate. With a little planning, it can be fun and emotionally rewarding. Involve the family in menu planning, grocery shopping, setting the table, and even cleaning up. Cooking is a wonderful way to spend time together, and helping hands make creating a delicious, nutritious dinner a snap.

This hearty meal can be started ahead of time or made on the spot with the family in the kitchen. Chop the meat loaf ingredients, then let the kids mix it up. Let them wash and dry the lettuce, whisk the salad dressing, shuck the corn, prepare the biscuit dough, and cut out the biscuits. This recipe for carrots is fail-proof, and who wouldn't love spreading whipped topping on a Hershey bar pie!

The leftovers in this chapter make a great lunch-box or brown-bag meal. At the end of a full day of school and work, there is nothing better for the family soul than a hot, delicious supper.

Cheesy Meat Loaf

¼ cup finely chopped onion

½ cup finely chopped celery

2 teaspoons minced garlic

1 teaspoon dried parsley

2 teaspoons Creole seasoning

¼ teaspoon black pepper

1 teaspoon chili powder

1 teaspoon cumin

¾ cup salsa

3 eggs

1½ pounds lean ground beef or mix of lean ground beef and ground turkey

¾ cup dry bread crumbs

½ pound mozzarella cheese, sliced

Heat oven to 350°.

Place all ingredients, except cheese, in a large mixing bowl. Mix well with hands.

Transfer half of mixture to a 9- by 5-inch loaf pan. Place cheese on top, then cover with the rest of the meat mixture.

Bake for 60–70 minutes, or until a meat thermometer reads 170°.

Let meat loaf rest in pan for 20 minutes.

Serve.

Yield: 8 servings

Kitchen Notes

- Meat loaf sandwiches are a lunch-box favorite. Place leftover meat loaf in a Parmesan Cheese Biscuit (page 42) for a special treat.

- To save time, buy large quantities of onions, celery, and garlic. Chop and freeze for the next meat loaf meal.

- If you don't have commercially made bread crumbs on hand, place stale bread in the food processor and pulse until crumbs are fine.

Cheesy Meat Loaf (page 38), Carrot French Fries (page 40), and Parmesan Cheese Biscuits (page 42)

Carrot French Fries

2 pounds carrots, peeled

3 tablespoons butter, melted

2 teaspoons finely chopped fresh rosemary (optional)

½ teaspoon sugar

½ teaspoon salt

¼ teaspoon black pepper

Preheat oven to 425°. Line a jelly-roll pan with parchment paper.

Cut 1 carrot in half crosswise. Next, cut each half in half lengthwise. Finally, cut each half in half lengthwise again. You will end up with 8 sticks from the carrot. Repeat with the other carrots.

In the mixing bowl, combine carrot sticks, butter, rosemary (if using), sugar, salt, and pepper. Stir with a rubber spatula until carrot sticks are evenly coated with all other ingredients.

Dump carrots onto pan. Spread sticks out as much as possible. Bake until carrots are tender and well browned, about 20 minutes. Serve carrot fries hot or at room temperature.

Yield: 8 servings

Creamed Corn

2 tablespoons butter

½ onion, finely chopped

3 tablespoons flour

1¾ cups milk

1 teaspoon sugar

Salt and black pepper, to taste

2½ cups corn, fresh (4 or 5 ears, cut off the cob) or frozen kernels

Melt butter in a skillet and sauté onion until translucent, about 5 minutes.

Add flour and stir.

With a wire whisk, gradually add milk and cook over medium heat until thickened.

Stir in sugar, salt, and pepper, then add corn. Serve warm.

Yield: 6–8 servings

Kitchen Note

- To scrape kernels off the cob, hold corn upright on a cutting board and, using a utility knife, cut downward.

Dynamite Orange-Almond Salad

½ teaspoon salt

Black pepper, to taste

2 tablespoons sugar

4 tablespoons vinegar

¼ cup oil

6 drops Tabasco sauce

2 tablespoons chopped fresh parsley

½ cup sliced almonds

3 tablespoons sugar

1 bag (12 ounces) mixed greens

2 green onions, chopped

1 15-ounce can mandarin oranges, drained

For dressing, combine first seven ingredients (from salt through parsley). Whisk until well blended.

For glazed almonds, combine almonds and sugar in a small skillet. Heat on low and stir constantly until sugar is dissolved and almonds are well coated. Sugar can caramelize quickly and burn—watch carefully!

Pour onto waxed paper to cool.

Once cooled, break into small pieces.

To serve the salad, combine greens, onions, and oranges in a large salad bowl.

Pour dressing over salad and toss to combine.

Sprinkle glazed almonds on top and serve.

Yield: 6–8 servings

Kitchen Notes

- We love it with crumbled blue cheese and dried cherries on top.
- To save time, glaze almonds and make dressing ahead.

Parmesan Cheese Biscuits

2 cups all-purpose flour plus more as needed

¼ teaspoon baking soda

1 tablespoon baking powder

1 teaspoon salt

6 tablespoons shortening

¾ cup buttermilk

1 cup shredded Parmesan cheese

Preheat oven to 400°.

Sift dry ingredients into a large bowl.

Cut in shortening with a pastry blender or fork until mixture has the texture of coarse meal.

Add buttermilk and mix with a wooden spoon, lightly but thoroughly.

Add a little more flour if dough is too sticky.

Roll dough out ½ inch thick on a lightly floured surface or pastry cloth.

Cut dough using a 2-inch biscuit cutter.

Sprinkle with cheese.

Place biscuits on a baking sheet and bake until golden brown, 10–12 minutes.

Yield: 12 biscuits

Kitchen Notes

- Biscuits can be made with small, medium, or large cutters, depending on your preference. Use a large one to fashion the perfect biscuit for a meat loaf sandwich.

- Cut out biscuits, place on a sheet pan, and freeze. Once frozen, store biscuits in a plastic storage bag and use as needed.

- To save time, buy high-quality shredded Parmesan.

- To make your own buttermilk, use 1 tablespoon of whole milk, add 1 tablespoon of vinegar, and let sit for a couple of minutes.

- Use your fingers to "cut" the butter into the flour. The object is to rub the butter into the flour so it has a crumblike texture.

Hooray! For Hershey Bar Pie

1 Chocolate Wafer Pie Crust (page 166)

½ cup milk

20 large marshmallows

6 Hershey bars (1.94 ounces each), with almonds or plain

1 8-ounce carton nondairy whipped topping

Prepare crust, setting aside 2 tablespoons crushed cookies to sprinkle over top of pie.

Put milk and marshmallows in a saucepan over low heat, stirring constantly. When marshmallows are melted, add Hershey bars.

Stir until melted and blended.

Pour mixture into cooled pie crust.

Refrigerate for at least 30 minutes.

When pie is set, spread with whipped topping.

Sprinkle with reserved crushed cookies.

Yield: 6–9 servings

Kitchen Note

● To save time, buy an Oreo cookie pie crust, found in the baking aisle of your local grocery store.

Not-So-Mundane Monday Night

"Here's the Beef" Kebabs

Broccoli Trees

Volcano Potatoes

Golden Cheese Wedges

A+ Brownies

We don't believe in "mundane Mondays," so we get a jump on that evening's supper by planning ahead on Sunday. We collectively ease out of our weekend frame of mind by gently turning our attention toward the new week. During the school year, this means washing off the weekend with a good hot bath, collecting schoolbooks, thinking about homework, and planning meals. For Monday's dinner, we start the night before by marinating the beef, trimming the broccoli trees, boiling the potatoes, and making the brownies. (And, of course, we never mind if a brownie or two disappears or finds its way into a Monday lunch box.) We wait until just before supper to make the Golden Cheese Wedges. These biscuits are simple and fun to make—a tasty treat or reward for preparing a not-so-mundane Monday night dinner.

"Here's the Beef" Kebabs

MARINADE:

2 cloves garlic, finely chopped

1 tablespoon sesame oil

1 teaspoon honey

1 tablespoon lemon juice

½ cup soy sauce

KEBABS:

1½ pounds London broil or round cut, cut into 1-inch cubes

10 skewers

2 tablespoons dried rosemary, if not using sprigs

1 large green bell pepper, cored and cut into 1-inch pieces

1 large red bell pepper, cored and cut into 1-inch pieces

5 small onions, sliced in half

10 fresh mushrooms

10 sprigs fresh rosemary

Mix all marinade ingredients together.

Place meat in marinade, cover, and refrigerate for at least 2 hours, or overnight, turning the meat occasionally for an even coating. This may be done in a zip-top bag.

If using bamboo skewers, make sure to soak them in warm water for at least 30 minutes before using.

Sprinkle rosemary leaves, if using instead of sprigs, all over marinade.

Assemble kebabs by alternately spearing beef, peppers, onions, and mushrooms on skewers.

Twist 1 rosemary sprig around each skewer.

Grill kebabs, turning occasionally, until cooked to desired doneness.

Yield: 8–10 servings

Kitchen Notes

- You can often find ready-made kebabs in your local market. Just make the marinade.
- Use a garlic press to crush the garlic cloves.

"Here's the Beef" Kebabs (opposite), Broccoli Trees (page 48), and Volcano Potatoes (page 49)

Broccoli Trees

1 pound broccoli florets with 2-inch stems

4 teaspoons grated Parmesan cheese

2 teaspoons lemon-pepper seasoning

Peel any thick fibrous skin from broccoli stems. Cut "trees" by separating florets with knife and slicing down through stems.

Place in a steamer over simmering water. Cover. Steam for 8–10 minutes, or until stems are tender and broccoli is bright green. Drain.

Combine cheese and seasoning in small dish. Sprinkle over broccoli.

Yield: 6 servings

Kitchen Note

● This amusing presentation encourages kids to eat this healthy vegetable.

Volcano Potatoes

6 large potatoes

2 egg yolks

4 tablespoons butter plus more for greasing dish

1 teaspoon salt, or more or less to taste

¼ teaspoon black pepper, or more or less to taste

⅓ cup milk

6 tablespoons grated Cheddar cheese

Peel potatoes, and then cut each into 4 pieces.

Put potatoes into a large saucepan and add enough cold water to cover them by 1 inch.

Bring to a boil over high heat. Reduce heat until water simmers or bubbles slightly. Cover saucepan and cook potatoes for 20 minutes.

After 20 minutes, insert a fork into a potato piece. If it goes in easily, potatoes are done.

Place a colander in the sink and drain potatoes.

Put potatoes back into saucepan. Add egg yolks to hot potatoes. Use a hand mixer or standing mixer to beat potatoes and yolks until smooth.

Add 4 tablespoons butter, salt, pepper, and milk. Beat potatoes with mixer until light and fluffy.

Preheat oven to 350°. Lightly grease a medium baking dish with butter. Spoon 6–8 mounds mashed potatoes, each about 3 inches high, into baking dish.

Use a rubber spatula to shape potatoes into volcano shapes. Use a spoon to make a crater in the top of each volcano.

Fill each volcano with 1 tablespoon cheese. Bake volcano potatoes until cheese melts and potatoes are lightly browned.

Remove potatoes from oven. Use a metal spatula to loosen potatoes carefully from bottom of baking dish. Lift them directly onto each dinner plate and serve.

Yield: 6–8 servings

Kitchen Note

- We grew up creating lakes of gravy in our mounds of mashed potatoes. In this recipe, we fill the crater with cheese.

Golden Cheese Wedges

2 cups all-purpose flour

1 tablespoon baking powder

¼ teaspoon salt

6 tablespoons cold butter, cut into chunks

⅔ cup milk

½ cup (2 ounces) shredded Cheddar cheese

Preheat oven to 400°.

Lightly grease a 9-inch glass pie plate.

Combine flour, baking powder, and salt in the bowl of a food processor or electric mixer. Add butter in chunks, and pulse until mixture resembles coarse meal.

Add milk and pulse until just combined.

Turn dough out onto a lightly floured surface and pat into a round shape about ⅓ inch thick. Place dough in pie plate and cut into wedges, not cutting all the way through.

Cover with cheese and bake for 15 minutes, or until lightly brown on top and cooked through. If cheese hasn't browned, broil for 1 minute.

Yield: 8 servings

Kitchen Notes

- When working with dough, coat your hands and work surface with extra flour to prevent sticking.
- Cheese wedges are delicious served warm with butter and jelly.

A+ Brownies

1 cup butter

4 1-ounce squares unsweetened chocolate

4 eggs

2 teaspoons vanilla extract

2 cups sugar

½ teaspoon salt

½ teaspoon baking powder

1 cup all-purpose flour

1 12-ounce package miniature chocolate chips

Preheat oven to 325°. Grease a 9- by 11-inch pan and set aside.

Slowly melt butter and chocolate over low heat in a double boiler, stirring occasionally. This can also be done in a microwave. Place butter and chocolate in a microwave-safe dish. Microwave on high for 1 minute. Check and stir. If not melted, continue to microwave in 30-second intervals until smooth.

Put eggs and vanilla extract in a mixing bowl and whisk.

Add sugar, salt, baking powder, and flour and blend using a hand mixer or standing mixer until combined.

Carefully add melted chocolate mixture. Mix until thoroughly blended.

Fold in chocolate chips.

Pour mixture into pan and bake for 25–30 minutes, or until a wooden pick inserted in center of brownies comes out clean.

Let cool and cut into squares.

Yield: 10–12 servings

Kitchen Notes

- Be careful not to overcook the brownies, as they continue cooking when removed from the oven.
- For the creative cook: Substitute your choice of miniature flavored chips for chocolate chips.
- When saving for school or office snacks, wrap brownies individually in plastic wrap and freeze.

Ring the Dinner Bell

Tasty, Tender Pork Tenderloin

Carrot Coins

Creamy Dreamy Broccoli-Parmesan Risotto

Grandmother's Dinner Rolls

Myers's Favorite Buttermilk Pie

I was named for my grandmother, Helen Todd, and because I was her namesake, we always had a special bond. My brothers and sister loved her dearly, and she adored each of them, but I can't help thinking that sharing her name made me just a little more special. Being in the kitchen with Grandmother was always one of my favorite pastimes. I considered cooking with her preferable to even the most thrilling game my brothers and sister would think up. She lived some 90 miles away from us, but we stayed with her often. The little two-bedroom house opened its doors to magically accommodate six children when our parents would take off for some business meeting or convention. I would walk in the back door and hear the mixer going and breathe in the aroma of something wonderful baking in the oven.

She was an accomplished Southern cook, and when she rang the dinner bell, you were assured of a hot, tasty meal of roast beef, pork roast, or fried chicken; at least three vegetables; and always a pan of cornbread *and* a pan of rolls. Grandmother's dinner rolls have always been one of my favorites. After she died, my mom and sister and I tried and tried to make these rolls, but we never could. It seemed that without her patient and knowing hands, the dough had a will of its own. When writing this book, I was thumbing through her recipe box and found a note saying the secret to her rolls is refrigerating the covered dough overnight. People say when a loved one dies they are still with you, and when I read her note, I knew it was true. Carol, Mom, and I are proud that we can now "successfully" make Grandmother's Dinner Rolls—and we know she is proud of us.

Tasty, Tender Pork Tenderloin

1½ pounds pork tenderloin

3 tablespoons soy sauce

3 tablespoons hoisin sauce

2 tablespoons vegetable oil

½ teaspoon salt

1½ teaspoons sugar

2 tablespoons butter

Put tenderloin in a gallon-size zip-top bag. Add soy sauce, hoisin sauce, oil, salt, and sugar. Marinate tenderloin in the refrigerator for at least 2 hours.

Preheat oven to 500°.

Put tenderloin in a roasting pan.

Place in oven for 9 minutes.

Turn meat and roast for 9 minutes more, until internal temperature reaches 155°.

Remove from oven and allow to sit for 2–3 minutes.

Slice meat across the grain into thin slices.

Add butter to pan drippings and stir well.

Drizzle over meat.

Yield: 6 servings

Kitchen Notes

- Pork can marinate overnight, if desired.
- Pork tenderloin has very little fat and cooks well at this high temperature.
- For juicier meat, allow the tenderloin to rest for a few minutes after cooking and before slicing.

Carrot Coins

10–12 medium-long, thin carrots, peeled and
     sliced into thin rounds

2 teaspoons sesame seeds

2 tablespoons butter

½ teaspoon salt

¼ teaspoon black pepper

2 teaspoons orange juice

2 tablespoons light brown sugar

½ cup water

Preheat oven to 375°.

Boil or steam carrots in a saucepan until tender but not mushy, about 10 minutes.

Drain carrots in a colander.

While carrots are cooking, you can toast the sesame
seeds. Spread sesame seeds on a sheet pan and toast for 5 minutes.

After carrots are cooked, sprinkle toasted sesame seeds on top.

Add remaining ingredients to saucepan.

Cook and stir over medium heat until mixture thickens and carrots are nicely coated with syrup.

Add more sugar and/or water, depending on how syrupy you like them.

Yield: 6–8 servings

Creamy Dreamy
Broccoli-Parmesan Risotto

1 onion, finely chopped

3 tablespoons olive oil

1½ cups uncooked short-grain (Arborio) or regular rice

6 cups chicken broth, warm

2 cups broccoli florets

1½ cups grated Parmesan cheese

½ teaspoon salt

In a heavy saucepan, sauté onion in oil until transparent. Add rice and cook over medium-high heat, stirring constantly, for about 2 minutes.

Reduce heat to medium-low and add 1 cup broth. Stir until completely absorbed by rice. Continue to add broth 1 cup at a time, constantly stirring, saving 1 cup for the end.

Once 5 cups broth have been thoroughly absorbed, stir in broccoli and final cup broth. Stir, stir, and stir for 5 minutes.

Add cheese and salt. The risotto should be creamy in consistency. Allow to stand for a minute or two, then enjoy.

Yield: 6–8 servings

Kitchen Notes

- For variety, substitute asparagus tips for broccoli.
- Time-saver: Buy pregrated Parmesan cheese.
- Risotto is a dish that requires patience, but the reward is worth the effort. Plan to stir constantly for about 20 to 25 minutes.

Grandmother's Dinner Rolls

½ cup sugar

½ cup vegetable shortening

2 cups milk

1 package active dry yeast

¼ cup water (105°–115°)

4 cups all-purpose flour

1 teaspoon baking soda

1 teaspoon salt

1 teaspoon baking powder

In a small pan on top of stove, melt sugar and shortening in milk. Cool.

Dissolve yeast in water.

When milk mixture cools, transfer it to a bowl. Add yeast and 2 cups flour.

Beat with a hand mixer or wooden spoon to get out the lumps.

Cover with a clean dish towel and let rise 45 minutes in a warm place.

Sift 1½ cups flour, baking soda, salt, and baking powder. Add to risen yeast-and-flour mixture.

Place dough in refrigerator, covered, overnight, or until ready to use.

Place dough on floured board or countertop.

Work additional flour into the sticky dough until it is the right consistency for rolling out.

With a floured rolling pin, roll out dough to ½-inch thickness. Cut rounds with a biscuit cutter, fold over, and place in a greased pan or on a cookie sheet. Let rise, covered, for 20 minutes before baking.

Bake at 400° until done, about 10–12 minutes.

Serve warm with honey or butter.

Yield: about 5 dozen rolls

Kitchen Notes

- Heat the milk, sugar, and shortening on low heat until the shortening melts. No boiling allowed! The finished product should be warm to the touch, like a baby's bath.

- The secret to these delicious rolls is refrigerating the covered dough overnight.

Myers's Favorite Buttermilk Pie

1 9-inch Homemade Pie Crust (page 167)
   or ready-made crust

1¼ cups sugar

½ cup butter, at room temperature

1 tablespoon flour

3 eggs, well beaten

¾ cup buttermilk, room temperature

1 tablespoon vanilla extract

Preheat oven to 500°.

Prepare crust according to directions.

Blend sugar, butter, and flour, using a mixer on low speed.

Add eggs, buttermilk, and vanilla extract. Mix until combined.

Pour into crust. Turn oven to 400°.

Place pie in oven and bake at 400° for 10 minutes.

Without opening the oven door, reduce temperature to 325° and bake for an additional
40–45 minutes.

Allow to cool before serving.

Yield: 8 servings

Kitchen Notes

- Use a hand mixer or stand mixer for blending.

- Setting a timer will help you remember to change the oven temperature. (It changes three times for this pie!)

- Before starting this recipe, it is very important to have all the ingredients at room temperature.

Everyone, Sit Down for Dinner

Wholesome Roasted Chicken

Sensational Succotash

Martin's Baked Sweet Potatoes

Cornbread Gems

Heavenly Butterfinger Dessert

"Everyone, sit down for dinner!" is what my mom said when we were growing up. And she meant *everyone*. We would wait for Richard to get home from football practice, Carol to finish practicing the piano, or Ben and me to end our tennis game. The age range at the dinner table was from 1 to 15, toddlers to teenagers, and everyone, even the little ones, had to share an experience or story from the day. It was loud and messy and more than a little rowdy, but it was our time to be together.

Roasted chicken was a family favorite then, as it is today. One of my cooking students is a blue-eyed 5-year-old named Sterling who claims that her father makes the best roasted chicken in the whole wide world. I happily accepted an invitation to watch this father-daughter duo make the ultimate comfort food. Sterling reached into a low kitchen drawer and found aprons for each of them. She pulled up a stool to help her father, Clark, find the seasonings. He held the chicken over the sink, and she seasoned it, layering the seasonings evenly before helping him put the bird in the roasting pan. It was apparent to her proud cooking teacher that Sterling and her father were "at home" in the family kitchen and had prepared this dish many times before. Leslie and I agree with Sterling that the best roasted chicken in the whole wide world is made when families cook together.

When my son, Martin, was a little boy, one of the first foods introduced to his toddler community at Montessori school was the sweet potato. He wanted them every night, and often I would oblige. His job was to pierce the potatoes with a fork and wrap them in foil. I would bake and peel them so he could mash the warm potatoes. Today, he is still a big fan of sweet potatoes.

Heavenly Butterfinger Dessert is an old recipe from Leslie's mom, and I agree that it is indeed heavenly. Leslie remembers it as the most requested dessert at pregame cheerleader dinners. How they cheered and jumped and tumbled after Butterfinger Dessert will remain one of life's mysteries.

Wholesome Roasted Chicken

Olive oil

Tabasco sauce

1 whole chicken (4–7 pounds)

Salt

Black pepper

Cayenne pepper

Paprika

Garlic powder

Lemon-pepper seasoning

Season-All or any seasoned salt

Fresh rosemary

Preheat oven to 325°. Position a rack in center of oven.

Cover the bottom of an ovenproof glass baking dish with oil. Add 8–10 drops Tabasco. Stir mixture. (This zips up the olive oil.)

Remove giblets and neck from inside chicken and discard. Rinse and lightly pat dry chicken. You want chicken damp so that the seasonings stick to it.

Hold chicken over the sink, breast down, and begin seasoning the back first.

The order of the seasonings is very important. Dust the chicken evenly and lightly with each one, beginning with the salt and continuing in this order: black pepper, cayenne pepper, paprika, garlic powder, lemon pepper, seasoned salt.

When you finish covering with seasoned salt, all the skin color of this side should have disappeared. Shake a little lemon pepper and rosemary in the oil mixture. Lay the seasoned side (which is the back) down in the pan with the oil mixture.

Repeat layering with seasonings on the front side. Make sure you pull and get around the legs. Top off with rosemary. Cover with aluminum foil.

Put in oven for 1 hour 45 minutes, or until a thermometer inserted in a breast registers 180°F and the juices run clear. After 1 hour, baste the chicken. (You can never overbaste.) Remove foil for the last 15 minutes of cooking to produce a crispy, glazed skin.

Yield: 4–6 servings

Kitchen Notes

- Arrange your seasonings in order before you begin dusting the chicken.

- Timing is everything! Place the chicken in the oven first. It will be ready by the time the rest of the dinner is prepared.

- It's easy to roast several chickens at a time, and they're the perfect treat to take to a friend or loved one. We love to do this when chickens are on sale.

Sensational Succotash

1½ cups lima beans, fresh or frozen

3 cups water

1½ cups corn kernels, fresh or frozen

1 tablespoon butter

½ teaspoon salt

¼ teaspoon black pepper

⅓ cup half and half

Put beans in a medium saucepan with water. Bring to a boil, reduce heat, cover, and simmer for about 10 minutes.

Turn heat back to high and add corn. When beans and corn have come to a boil, reduce heat to low and simmer, covered, for 5 more minutes. Remove from heat and drain in a colander.

Melt butter in a heavy skillet. Add beans, corn, salt, and pepper. Stir to combine. Pour in half and half and simmer slowly for about 15 more minutes.

Yield: 6–8 servings

Martin's Baked Sweet Potatoes

6 large sweet potatoes

4 tablespoons unsalted butter

2 teaspoons kosher salt

Preheat oven to 400°.

Wash sweet potatoes.

Pierce potatoes with a fork and wrap in aluminum foil. (For faster cooking, cut potatoes in large cubes and wrap in aluminum foil.)

Place potatoes on a baking sheet and bake until easily pierced with a fork, about 1 hour.

Peel potatoes while still hot.

Combine potatoes, butter, and salt in a large bowl. Mash with a potato masher until smooth. Serve immediately. (This can be prepared a day ahead and reheated.)

Yield: 6 servings

Kitchen Note

- Sweet potatoes are not just for the holiday season! They make a nutritious and delicious meal accompaniment any day of the year.

Cornbread Gems

½ cup yellow cornmeal

1 cup all-purpose flour

3 teaspoons baking powder

2 tablespoons sugar

1 teaspoon salt

¾ cup milk

1 egg, beaten

2 tablespoons butter, melted

Preheat oven to 425°.

Grease muffin tins.

Sift together all of the dry ingredients.

Gradually add milk, stirring well.

Add egg, then blend in butter.

Pour into muffin tins and bake for 15 minutes.

Yield: 1 dozen gems

Kitchen Notes

- If melting the butter in the micro-wave, place it in a glass dish and heat for 20 seconds.

- For an extraspecial treat, serve with butter and honey.

Heavenly Butterfinger Dessert

2 eggs

¼ cup butter, melted

2 cups confectioners' sugar

2 teaspoons vanilla extract

1 pint whipping cream

16 ounces angel food cake

6 (2.1 ounce) Butterfinger candy bars

In a medium mixing bowl, beat eggs with a whisk until blended.

Pour butter over eggs and whisk again until blended.

Add sugar and blend until smooth. Whisk in vanilla extract.

Using a hand mixer, whip cream until stiff.

Fold whipped cream into egg-and-butter mixture.

Break cake into small pieces.

Crush candy bars by pulsing in a food processor or by placing in a zip-top bag and rolling with a rolling pin.

In a 9- by 13-inch pan or trifle bowl, layer half the cake, half the creamed mixture, and half the candy bars. Repeat. Cover and refrigerate overnight.

Yield: 10–12 servings

Kitchen Notes

- Tearing the angel food cake into small pieces and crushing the candy bars are entertaining jobs for kids.

- For no-fail whipped cream, make sure the whipping cream is cold, and chill the mixing bowl and beaters in the freezer for 10 minutes. Beat continuously at medium speed with a stand mixer or hand mixer until the cream begins to stiffen. Be careful not to overbeat the cream because it will fall and become soupy.

It's Italian!

Homemade Pasta Dough

Unrivaled Red Sauce

Mighty Meatballs

Favorite Fettuccine Alfredo

Caesar Salad with Homemade Croutons

Crusty Italian Bread

Totally Terrific Tiramisu

Everyone loves Italian. The first time I taught this menu in a cooking class was for a private party of graduating high school seniors. They came to class with styled hair and dressed up like they were going out for a night on the town. They sat politely while Helen and I talked about cooking techniques and the tasty menu we were going to prepare. We are accustomed to lively, highly interactive hands-on classes, and the deadly silence and empty expressions gave us that sinking feeling that this was not going to work. We signaled each other that it was time to change gears. I told the girls that this was their class, and they could choose whether they would like to watch us demonstrate the menu or do it themselves. They looked around the room, reached a quick consensus, and said, "Let's do it." They grabbed aprons, stepped up to the countertop, and went to work. And the reward? A delicious Italian dinner.

Since then, I have taught this class to every age group from teenagers to golden agers, and it's hands-down one of the most popular classes we teach. Maybe it's because it takes more than one person to crank out the pasta, and it's a fun and entertaining activity, whether in cooking class or at home. The only equipment needed is a simple, inexpensive hand-crank pasta machine to transform a ball of dough into long, silky strands of pasta. The rest of the meal is easy to make. Choose from two delicious sauces, whip up the classic Caesar Salad with Homemade Croutons, bake a loaf of Crusty Italian Bread, and top it all off with a superdelicious and supereasy Totally Terrific Tiramisu.

Homemade Pasta Dough

3 cups white bread flour

1 teaspoon salt

4 large eggs, at room temperature

1 tablespoon olive oil

Place flour and salt in a bowl, and make a well in the center.

Beat eggs. Pour into well in center of flour. Add the olive oil.

Mix with a fork at first, then flour one of your hands and knead dough until it is uniform and smooth, about 5 minutes. Add a little more flour if dough seems unreasonably sticky.

Cover dough with a clean dish towel and let it rest at room temperature for 1 hour.

After dough has rested, turn it out onto a lightly floured surface and knead it for about 1 minute.

Divide dough into balls the size of a tight fist.

Begin feeding through a pasta machine, following the steps to make a long sheet.

Run dough through the cutting mode and cut into long, thin strands for spaghetti or slightly thicker strands for fettuccine. (Alternatively, you may cut the dough into any shape you like. For lasagna, you can either leave the sheets whole or cut into long, wide noodles—you name it!)

Cook pasta in a large saucepan with lightly salted boiling water until just done, about 5 minutes. Be careful not to overcook! Homemade pasta cooks much more quickly than the dried kind!

Yield: 6–8 servings (double amounts for lasagna)

NOTE: The pasta can be frozen after cutting into strands.

Kitchen Notes

- Once the pasta is cut into strands, drape them over a coat hanger to dry.

- The process of kneading converts the dough from being slightly sticky to more elastic. Before kneading, rub your hands with flour so the dough will not stick. With the heel of your hand, press the dough away from yourself, fold it over, and repeat the process several times. Start again forming it into a loose ball, then press and fold again. It takes 10 to 15 minutes of this continuous motion to make the dough smooth and elastic.

Unrivaled Red Sauce

2 tablespoons olive oil

1½ cups finely chopped yellow onion

2 teaspoons minced garlic (4 cloves)

½ teaspoon salt

2 teaspoons Italian seasoning

¼ teaspoon ground black pepper

1 28-ounce can tomato puree

2 15-ounce cans tomato sauce

1 6-ounce can tomato paste

1½ cups water

1 teaspoon sugar

Heat oil in a large stockpot over medium heat.

Add onions, garlic, salt, Italian seasoning, and pepper and cook until onions are soft and transparent, about 4 minutes.

Place tomato puree in stockpot. Stir with a wooden spoon.

Add tomato sauce, tomato paste, water, and sugar to the pot and stir well.

Bring to a simmer over medium-high heat.

Lower heat to medium-low and simmer, uncovered, for 45 minutes, stirring occasionally with a long-handled wooden spoon.

Using potholders, remove stockpot from heat and use sauce as needed. Once it has cooled, you can store this sauce in an airtight container in the refrigerator for up to 4 days or freeze it up to 3 months.

Yield: 8 cups

Kitchen Notes

- Chop the garlic or press it through a garlic press. One clove of garlic equals ½ teaspoon of pressed garlic. For this recipe, you will need 4 cloves. We love the garlic press!

- This sauce freezes well.

Homemade Pasta (page 70), Unrivaled Red Sauce (page 71), and Mighty Meatballs (opposite)

Mighty Meatballs

8 cups Unrivaled Red Sauce (page 71)

2 large eggs

1½ pounds lean ground turkey or lean ground beef

½ cup finely chopped yellow onion

1 teaspoon minced garlic

2 teaspoons Italian seasoning

½ teaspoon ground black pepper

2 teaspoons yellow mustard

2 teaspoons ketchup

½ teaspoon salt

½ teaspoon Creole seasoning

½ cup Italian-style bread crumbs

All-purpose flour for coating

2 tablespoons olive oil

Pour sauce into a large heavy pot.

Bring to a simmer over medium heat and stir.

Place all remaining meatball ingredients except flour and oil in a mixing bowl. Stir well.

Using your hands, shape meat to form meatballs.

Roll lightly in flour.

Heat oil in a skillet over medium-high heat and cook meatballs until lightly browned on all sides.

Carefully place meatballs into sauce, one by one.

Simmer, uncovered, for 10 minutes before stirring. When meatballs rise to the top, it's okay to stir.

Stir sauce and meatballs. Simmer for an additional 20 minutes and stir occasionally.

Remove sauce from heat and serve over cooked pasta.

Yield: 6–8 servings

Kitchen Notes

- Use your hands to thoroughly mix the meat with the seasonings, then roll it into balls a bit smaller than Ping-Pong balls.
- Place the flour in a shallow bowl and roll the meatballs in the flour to coat all sides.

Favorite Fettuccine Alfredo

6 quarts water

1 tablespoon salt

1 pound fettuccine

2 cups heavy cream

Salt and black pepper, to taste

Pinch of ground nutmeg

2 cups (8 ounces) grated Parmesan cheese plus more for sprinkling

Pour water into a large pot and add salt. Set the pot over high heat, cover with the lid, and bring water to a boil. Remove lid. Slowly and carefully add pasta, then stir it with a long-handled fork. Boil pasta, uncovered, until al dente (tender, but still firm to the bite), about 9 minutes, or according to the package directions. Stir occasionally to prevent from sticking.

While pasta is boiling, pour cream into a medium saucepan and add salt, pepper, and nutmeg. Set pan over high heat and bring cream to a gentle boil. Reduce heat to low, stirring occasionally with a wooden spoon until slightly thickened, about 5 minutes. Remove pan from heat and set aside until pasta is ready.

Set a colander in the sink. Have potholders ready. When pasta is cooked, pour contents of the pot into the colander. Drain quickly, shaking colander, and dump pasta back into the pot.

Add warm cream to pasta. Add cheese. Using 2 wooden spoons, toss until ingredients are well blended. Allow about 2 minutes for pasta to absorb some of the sauce.

Spoon pasta onto plates. Sprinkle with additional grated cheese. Serve immediately.

Yield: 6 servings

Kitchen Notes

- When the cream comes to a slight boil, immediately turn the heat to low.

- This sauce is good on any noodle.

Caesar Salad with Homemade Croutons

CROUTONS:

1 cup olive oil

½ cup (2 ounces) freshly grated Parmesan cheese

2 tablespoons minced garlic

1 teaspoon chopped fresh oregano

1 teaspoon chopped fresh thyme

1 pound day-old bread, preferably sourdough, sliced and cut into 1-inch cubes (about 4 cups)

CAESAR VINAIGRETTE:

1 egg, pasteurized in shell

4 tablespoons fresh lemon juice

1 tablespoon minced garlic

1 teaspoon Worcestershire sauce

¼ teaspoon red-pepper flakes

1 tablespoon Dijon mustard

2 teaspoons anchovy paste

¾ cup peanut oil

¼ cup extra-virgin olive oil

¼ cup (1 ounce) freshly grated Parmesan cheese

Kosher salt and freshly ground black pepper, to taste

SALAD:

3 heads baby romaine or 1 large head romaine lettuce, washed and patted dry

Freshly grated Parmesan cheese

TO MAKE CROUTONS:

Preheat oven to 350°.

In a medium bowl, combine oil, cheese, garlic, oregano, and thyme. Add bread and toss, coating all the croutons.

Arrange croutons in a single layer on a baking sheet and bake until golden, turning to brown on all sides, about 15–20 minutes. Cool and store in a cool, dry place.

TO MAKE CAESAR VINAIGRETTE:

In a medium bowl, whisk together egg, lemon juice, garlic, Worcestershire sauce, red-pepper flakes, mustard, and anchovy paste.

While continuing to whisk, add oils in a slow, steady stream until dressing is thoroughly combined.

Stir in cheese and season with salt and pepper. Refrigerate in a covered container. When ready to use, whisk again.

TO ASSEMBLE SALAD:

Tear lettuce into bite-size pieces and place in a large salad bowl.

Toss with enough Caesar Vinaigrette to lightly coat.

Arrange on salad plates and sprinkle with croutons and a little cheese, if desired.

Yield: 8–10 servings salad; 2 cups vinaigrette

Kitchen Notes

- Croutons can be made 4 to 5 days ahead of time and stored in a zip-top bag. You will use 6 cloves of garlic in this recipe.
- Use the freshest eggs. The lemon juice will temper the egg.
- Any leftover vinaigrette will keep in a covered container in the refrigerator for 3 days.

Crusty Italian Bread

1 package rapid-rise dry yeast

1 tablespoon sugar

1 cup warm water (105°–115°)

2½ cups bread flour

1½ teaspoons salt

1 teaspoon balsamic vinegar

2 tablespoons cornmeal (or enough to sprinkle in loaf pans)

¼ cup extra-virgin olive oil with 1 teaspoon salt, warmed

Preheat oven to 425°.

Dissolve yeast and sugar in warm water until bubbly, 5–10 minutes.

Place flour and salt in a food processor with a metal blade in place and pulse to mix. Add dissolved yeast and vinegar. Process 15–20 seconds.

Turn dough out onto an unfloured, lightly oiled board and hand-knead a few times by pressing and folding dough, using the heel of your hand.

Place dough in a warm, oiled bowl and turn to coat. Cover and allow to rise until doubled, 45 minutes to an hour. Punch dough down, cut into halves, and form each half into a cylinder.

Place halves in 2 greased French bread pans that have been lightly sprinkled with cornmeal. Glaze with salted oil. Allow to rise until doubled again, 30–45 minutes.

Bake 15–20 minutes, or until golden brown and crusty.

Serve with lots of butter.

Yield: 2 loaves

Kitchen Notes

- When adding warm water to the yeast, the water should feel like a baby's bathwater.

- When the yeast is bubbly, it is ready to be added to the flour and salt. Add the vinegar, then push the on button on the food processor. Let it run for about 20 seconds.

- After the dough is shaped into cylinders, you may freeze the loaves by covering them with plastic wrap and placing in a plastic storage bag. The dough may be frozen up to a month.

Totally Terrific Tiramisu

2 ounces dark chocolate

1 cup mascarpone

8 ounces cream cheese, softened

2 cups sour cream

½ cup sugar

1½ cups brewed decaf coffee (regular works, too!)

20 ladyfingers

Finely grate chocolate with a grater or food processor.

Combine mascarpone, cream cheese, sour cream, and sugar in a large bowl and whisk until smooth and thoroughly combined.

Pour coffee into a shallow dish. Pull ladyfingers apart. Dip each ladyfinger lightly into coffee.

Place ladyfingers along the sides of a 2-quart glass dish, then cover bottom with ladyfingers, round sides down, making sure they fit snugly.

Cover ladyfingers with a layer of cheese mixture and sprinkle with a little grated chocolate.

Repeat layers, finishing with cheese mixture. Sprinkle this with remaining chocolate and chill in the refrigerator for 2–3 hours.

Yield: 6–8 servings

Kitchen Notes

- Instead of one large dessert, you can make several mini tiramisus.
- Be sure to dip ladyfingers "lightly." If you dunk them, they may become too heavy and fall apart.

South of the Border

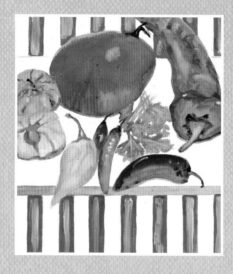

Sour Cream Eat Ya Enchiladas

Fiesta Rice

Tempting Taco Quesadillas

Mostly Mango Salsa

Nothing-to-It Nacho Breadsticks

Mexican Made-in-the-Pan Chocolate Cake

Just announcing "We're having Mexican food!" makes suppertime a fiesta at my house. When I was growing up, this was a festive favorite pregame supper for my high school cheerleading team. My family and friends still cheer for this sensational south-of-the-border supper that can and should be started the day before. Chicken breasts for enchiladas and the ground beef for tacos can be cooked and seasoned beforehand. And there are plenty of tasks for kids of all ages. Children delight in grating cheese and are adept at filling and rolling the enchiladas. Mostly Mango Salsa is an *At Home Café* invention by my four kids and me, and making it has become a family ritual. The Mexican chocolate cake is a no-mess, one-dish wonder and a dessert you'll make again and again.

Ever since I was introduced to the distinctive taste of tomatillos, I've been making tomatillo salsa. Then, a couple of years ago, someone gave me some ripe, delicious mangoes, which I used to re-create a tropical salsa I had tasted on an island vacation. I added the mangoes to my salsa recipe, and it was scrumptious. My kids liked it so much that it became one of their favorite dishes to make themselves, and they are forever sending me to the market in search of ripe mangoes. One "mangoless" day, they even created a batch of salsa with kiwifruit, and that was delicious, too.

One of the first recipes Helen taught in Montessori school was Mexican Made-in–the-Pan Chocolate Cake. It's a fantastic recipe for the beginning cook and a favorite of my daughter, Annie. My husband and I came home from a dinner party late one night to find Annie and her sleepover company busy in the kitchen making this cake. I was delighted to know that she has inherited at least some of my qualities and finds a wooden spoon and a bowl more entertaining than television or computer games.

My kids often request taco quesadillas instead of sandwiches, and I am happy to oblige them. It's a favorite Saturday lunch for my sons William and Myers, so I always keep the ingredients on hand.

Sour Cream Eat Ya Enchiladas

6 boneless, skinless chicken breasts

Extra-virgin olive oil

Creole seasoning

2 tablespoons butter

4 tablespoons chopped onion

1 4.5-ounce can chopped green chiles

1 cup (8 ounces) sour cream

8 ounces cream cheese

12 flour tortillas (6-inch diameter)

12 ounces (3 cups) shredded Cheddar cheese

12 ounces (3 cups) shredded pepper Jack cheese

1 cup salsa

Preheat oven to 350°.

Coat chicken with oil and Creole seasoning.

Place in a baking dish and bake until tender, about 25 minutes. Cool and cut into cubes.

Coat a 9- by 13-inch (3-quart) glass baking dish with nonstick cooking spray.

In a saucepan, melt butter. Add onion and sauté until clear.

Add chiles, sour cream, and cream cheese, stirring constantly until smooth and well blended. Mix in cubed chicken.

Spoon 2–3 tablespoons of mixture down the center of each tortilla.

Top each tortilla evenly with cheeses and salsa.

Fold 1 side over filling, then roll and place seam side down in prepared baking dish.

Spoon remaining cheese and salsa over filled tortillas. Cover with foil.

Bake for 25–30 minutes, or until hot and bubbly.

Remove foil and return to oven and bake, uncovered, for an additional 5 minutes.

Yield: 6 servings

Fiesta Rice

1 large onion, finely chopped

2 cloves garlic, minced, or 1 teaspoon
garlic powder

4 tablespoons olive oil

1½ cups rice, uncooked

4 cups water

2 8-ounce cans tomato sauce

1 tablespoon chili powder

1 teaspoon salt

½ teaspoon black pepper

1 cup (4 ounces) shredded Cheddar
cheese

2 cups (8 ounces) shredded Monterey
Jack cheese

Preheat oven to 450°.

In a medium saucepan, sauté onion and garlic in oil until tender.

Add rice and continue to cook until golden color.

Add water, tomato sauce, chili powder, salt, and pepper. Cover and simmer for 20–25 minutes.

Coat 2-quart casserole with nonstick cooking spray or grease with butter.

Spoon rice mixture into casserole and top with cheeses.

Bake for 5–8 minutes, or until cheese bubbles.

Yield: 6–8 servings

Kitchen Note

● Our guests always go back for seconds, so we usually double this recipe.

Tempting Taco Quesadillas

1 pound ground beef

1 tablespoon chopped fresh cilantro (optional)

¾ cup water

1 package taco seasoning

1 package soft flour tortillas (8-inch diameter)

2 avocados, peeled and sliced (optional)

1 cup (4 ounces) finely shredded pepper Jack or Mexican blend cheese

1 cup (4 ounces) shredded Cheddar cheese

Taco sauce

Brown beef in a skillet over medium-high heat, stirring to break up any lumps. Carefully drain and discard any excess oil.

Add cilantro (if using), water, and taco seasoning to beef and stir to combine. Bring mixture to a boil. Reduce heat to a simmer and cook, uncovered, stirring occasionally, for 10 minutes.

Preheat oven to 425° and coat a baking sheet with nonstick cooking spray.

Spoon some of the meat mixture over half of each tortilla.

Top with avocados and cheese.

Drizzle with taco sauce.

Fold tortillas in half and, using a metal spatula, transfer to baking sheet.

Bake for 15–20 minutes, or until heated through and cheese is melted.

Yield: 6 servings

Kitchen Notes

- There are no rules! When assembling the quesadillas, add as much meat, cheese, or other ingredients as you like, just as long as the tortilla folds over.

- Customize quesadillas with your favorite cheeses and meats.

Tempting Taco Quesadillas (opposite), and Mostly Mango Salsa (page 84)

Mostly Mango Salsa

2 large mangoes, peeled and chopped

8 tomatillos, finely chopped

1 orange or yellow bell pepper, cored, seeded, and finely chopped

½ cup finely chopped cilantro

½ cup finely chopped red onion

¼ teaspoon salt

1 teaspoon ground cumin

Juice of 1 lime

Place all ingredients in a medium bowl and stir until thoroughly combined.

Add more salt and lime juice as desired.

Yield: 3 cups

Nothing-to-It Nacho Breadsticks

¾ cup spicy nacho-flavored tortilla chips (about 30 chips), finely crushed

1 11-ounce can refrigerated breadsticks

Preheat oven to 375°.

Place crushed chips in a shallow dish or pan.

Separate breadstick dough into strips.

Roll both sides of each piece of dough in chips, pressing to adhere slightly.

Twist each strip twice. Place strips on a large ungreased cookie sheet, pressing ends down firmly.

Bake for 13–15 minutes, or until golden brown. Serve warm.

Yield: 12 breadsticks

Kitchen Note

- Place tortilla chips in a plastic storage bag and crush with your fingers.

Mexican Made-in-the-Pan Chocolate Cake

1¼ cups all-purpose flour

⅓ cup unsweetened cocoa

1 cup sugar

½ teaspoon salt

¾ teaspoon baking soda

½ teaspoon cinnamon

1 cup water

⅓ cup canola oil or vegetable oil

1 teaspoon vanilla extract

1 teaspoon cider vinegar or white vinegar

Preheat oven to 325°.

Lightly grease an 8-inch-square cake pan.

Sift flour, cocoa, sugar, salt, baking soda, and cinnamon into pan.

Mix it slowly, taking turns with a fork and a soup spoon, until it is completely light brown.

When dry ingredients are all mixed, make 4 dents with a spoon—2 large and 2 small—in mixture.

Pour water into 1 of the large dents.

Pour oil into the other large dent.

Pour vanilla extract into 1 of the small dents.

Pour vinegar into the other small dent.

Begin stirring slowly with a fork in little circles to get all of the dry parts wet.

As mixture turns into batter, start mashing it down with the fork. After you mash a few times, scrape the bottom and stir. Do this again many times: Mash, scrape, and stir.

When batter is smooth, scrape sides once more with a rubber spatula and spread batter into place.

Bake for 30 minutes.

Cool cake in pan for 30 minutes before cutting it into squares.

Yield: 8 servings

Unfancy French

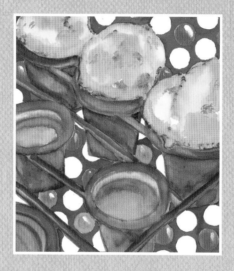

Bistro Brown Sugar–Glazed Brie

Crêpes!!!

Chicken & Mushroom Crêpes

Freshest French Green Beans (Haricots Verts)

Mixed Baby Greens with Fabulous French Dressing

Paris Popovers

Your Very Own Chocolate Soufflé with Vanilla Ice Cream

For some cooks, the thought of a French dinner menu summons notions of delicate sauces, difficult classic preparations, and a formal table. But when I think of French food, I think of warm, inviting neighborhood bistros where the food is simple, nourishing, and always delicious. Leslie and I use this menu not only to feed our families and entertain our friends but also as a way to teach our students about France while they're learning to cook. While we are flipping crêpes and beating egg whites, we talk about the Eiffel Tower, the Louvre, fields of lavender, French cheeses, and the special emphasis the French people place on food. It's a vivid example that cooking and culture are inseparable, and kids enthusiastically eat foods not normally found on the family table once they've learned their history and origin. It's been our experience that the best way to get kids to eat green beans and other vegetables is to let them do the cooking.

This versatile menu can go from everyday to elegant and reminds me of a visit with friends Karen and Todd Ruppert and their daughters Kierstin and Kali in Baltimore last year. Leslie and I were in the area for a book signing, and the Rupperts had a beautiful party for us featuring foods cooked from our book. A chef prepared the crêpes to order, and I must say they were scrumptious. Each guest was invited to choose from an incredible array of ingredients to create his or her perfect crêpe. Our hostess served the Bistro Brown Sugar–Glazed Brie as well. This brie recipe is a favorite that we both serve in our homes and take to parties when it's our turn to bring an appetizer. It's quick, easy, and always a hit.

Keep this menu in mind for an elegant dinner party, French Day at school, or just a fun family supper. It's a great opportunity to introduce your child to new words and discuss a different culture!

Bistro Brown Sugar–Glazed Brie

1 -pound wheel brie, rind removed

2 cups light brown sugar

1 cup pecans, chopped (optional)

¼ cup butter, melted

Crackers

Preheat oven to 300°.

Place brie on a pie plate.

Mix brown sugar and pecans (if using), place on top of cheese, and drizzle with butter.

Place in oven and heat for 8–10 minutes, or until cheese melts.

Serve immediately with crackers.

Yield: 8 servings

Kitchen Notes

- This delicious cheese recipe can be made with the rind on or off.
- Melting butter in the microwave, about 30–40 seconds for ¼ cup, is a time-saver.

Crêpes!!!

3 large eggs

1½ cups milk

1 cup plus 2 tablespoons all-purpose flour

1 teaspoon sugar (1 tablespoon for dessert crêpes)

2 tablespoons butter, melted

Put all ingredients in a blender in the order listed and blend until batter is smooth.

Remove the lid and scrape down blender sides with a rubber spatula.

Briefly blend mixture again.

Set covered blender in the refrigerator for at least 30 minutes or up to 2 days.

When ready to cook the crêpes, use a paper towel to spread about 1 teaspoon butter or vegetable oil in the bottom of an 8- or 9-inch nonstick skillet with low sides or a crêpe pan. Heat the skillet on a stove-top burner set at medium. Blend batter again to smooth it.

For the first crêpe, pour ¼ to ⅓ cup batter into a measuring cup to help gauge how much to use.

Cook each crêpe, following the steps below. Adjust the heat if they brown too quickly or too slowly.

Pour the batter into your heated pan. Immediately tilt and swirl the pan to evenly coat the bottom. This should take about 5 seconds.

Cook the crêpe on the first side for about 45 seconds, then quickly flip it with a spatula and cook the other side for about half as long.

Grasping the pan securely, swiftly invert it so the cooked crêpe will fall onto a large plate. Wipe the skillet with a paper towel and rub a little butter in the pan before cooking the next crêpe.

Yield: 12 crêpes

Crêpes!!! (page 89), Chicken & Mushroom Crêpes (opposite), and Freshest French Green Beans (page 92)

Chicken & Mushroom Crêpes

5 ounces fresh mushrooms, sliced

3 tablespoons butter, melted

⅓ cup all-purpose flour

1¼ cups chicken broth, reserved from cooking chicken

¾ cup heavy cream

⅓ cup dry cooking sherry

1 cup (4 ounces) shredded white Cheddar cheese

1 pound chicken, cooked and chopped (2 cups)

12 Crêpes!!! (page 89)

4 tablespoons (1 ounce) grated Parmesan cheese

Preheat oven to 375°.

Sauté mushrooms in butter until soft.

Add flour, broth, cream, sherry, and Cheddar, stirring well after each.

Blend until smooth.

Add 1 cup cream sauce to chicken.

Place 3 tablespoons chicken mixture in each crêpe, roll up, and place in buttered casserole dish.

Pour remaining sauce over crêpes and sprinkle with Parmesan.

Bake at 375° for 20 minutes.

Yield: 12 crêpes

Kitchen Notes

- To clean mushrooms, wipe with a damp paper towel.
- Whisk to remove any lumps from the cream sauce.
- Crêpes are thin but strong, making it easy to roll the chicken mixture inside.

Freshest French Green Beans
(Haricots Verts)

1 pound fresh green beans

5 cups cold water

1 teaspoon salt

1 tablespoon butter

Salt and black pepper, to taste

¼ cup heavy cream

Place beans in a colander and wash them under cool running water in the sink.

Snap off both ends of beans with your fingers.

Put water and salt into a medium saucepan. Bring to a rapid boil over medium-high heat.

Using tongs, carefully add beans to boiling water. Cover saucepan and simmer beans on medium-low heat for 10 minutes, or until crisp-tender.

Drain beans in the colander and then return beans to saucepan.

Add butter to saucepan and sprinkle with salt and pepper. Add cream and stir gently to coat beans well.

Spoon beans into a bowl and serve.

Yield: 6 servings

Kitchen Notes

- Remove tops and tails from the beans by snapping the ends off. Remove the string if there is one.

- Boiling beans gives them a bright color and plump texture.

- These beans can be cooked in the microwave. Place in a 1-quart microwave-safe dish and add 1 tablespoon of salt. Cover with plastic wrap and cook on high for about 8 minutes. Let stand for 2 minutes. Then add butter, salt, pepper, and cream and stir.

Mixed Baby Greens
with Fabulous French Dressing

1 cup walnuts, toasted and chopped

2 12-ounce bags mixed baby salad
greens

½ cup thinly sliced red onion

1 avocado, thinly sliced

Fabulous French Dressing (below)

Preheat oven to 400°.

Place walnuts in oven on a baking sheet, for about 10 minutes, or until toasted.

Place greens, onion, and avocado in a salad bowl.

Toss lightly with Fabulous French Dressing.

Sprinkle toasted walnuts on top. Serve.

Yield: 6–8 servings

FABULOUS FRENCH DRESSING

8 ounces garlic vinegar

2 teaspoons salt

1 teaspoon Tabasco sauce

⅛ teaspoon cayenne pepper (to nearly
cover surface)

1 teaspoon garlic powder

¼ teaspoon paprika

3 heaping teaspoons Dijon mustard

16 ounces (½ liter) olive oil

In a quart mason jar, mix vinegar, salt, Tabasco, pepper, garlic powder, and paprika together. Cover jar and shake well.

Open jar and add mustard to vinegar mixture. Cover jar and shake well.

Finally, open jar and add oil. Cover jar again and shake until oil and vinegar are well combined.

Yield: 3 cups

Paris Popovers

3 cups milk

3¾ cups all-purpose flour

1½ teaspoons salt

1 teaspoon baking powder

6 large eggs, at room temperature

Preheat oven to 450°.

Place milk in glass measuring cup and microwave for 1 minute, or until warm to the touch.

Sift flour, salt, and baking powder into a large mixing bowl.

Crack eggs into a mixing bowl and beat at medium speed for about 3 minutes, or until pale in color.

With the mixer on low speed, gradually add flour mixture and milk, then beat on medium speed for 2 minutes.

Allow batter to rest for about 30 minutes at room temperature.

Coat popover pan with nonstick cooking spray and fill cups almost to the top with batter.

Place popover pan on a baking sheet and bake for 15 minutes.

Turn down the temperature to 375° without opening oven and bake for 30 minutes or longer, or until golden brown.

Serve warm.

Yield: 12 popovers

Kitchen Notes

- Sift flour, baking powder, and salt mixture till free of lumps.

- Use a hand mixer or standing mixer.

- Set the timer for 15 minutes. When timer chimes, without opening the oven, change the temperature to 375° and bake for 30 more minutes. Total baking time is 45 minutes.

Your Very Own Chocolate Soufflé with Vanilla Ice Cream

¼ cup butter

½ cup sugar

1 cup semisweet chocolate chips

3 tablespoons heavy cream

1 tablespoon all-purpose flour

1 tablespoon vanilla extract

8 eggs, room temperature

2 scoops vanilla ice cream, softened

For this recipe, you will need eight 3-inch ramekins or ovenproof bowls.

Preheat oven to 375°.

Grease each ramekin with butter. Sprinkle in 1 teaspoon sugar.

Rotate ramekin to coat inside, then pour out excess sugar.

Combine chocolate chips, cream, flour, and vanilla extract in a double boiler and stir mixture over low heat until melted and smooth.

Keep mixture warm until you are ready to use it by leaving it over hot water, not on the burner.

Separate eggs, placing whites in a bowl.

Whisk yolks.

When yolks are blended, gradually whisk in several tablespoons of the melted chocolate mixture. Add slowly so it does not cook the eggs.

Repeat until half of the chocolate has been added, then whisk in the remaining chocolate at once.

Using an electric mixer, beat egg whites until stiff peaks form.

Using a rubber spatula, gently fold a fourth of the beaten egg whites into the chocolate mixture until just combined.

Continue folding in the remaining egg whites until well blended.

Working quickly but carefully, divide mixture among ramekins, filling each to ½ inch from the top.

Bake soufflés on a sheet pan in the center of oven until well puffed, about 12–15 minutes.

Remove soufflés from oven.

Using a spoon, carefully make a small slit in the top of each soufflé and fill with some softened vanilla ice cream.

Careful—the ramekins are very hot! Enjoy!

Yield: 8 servings

It's Greek
to Me!

Big Fat Greek Pizza

Pastitsio with Pizzazz!

Mom's Marvelous Chicken Phyllo

Tossed Greek Salad Bowl

Feta Pita Toast

The Very Best Baklava

Every time a child is christened in Leslie's family, out comes Mom's Marvelous Chicken Phyllo. This family tradition started, as many do, out of circumstance and need. For the christening of Leslie's first child, her mom offered to cook the brunch, not realizing her week had been long committed to working day and night on another event. So what is a modern grandmother to do? Mary Lynn Andrews pulled out one of the first recipes given to her as a young bride when she moved from New Orleans to the Mississippi river town of Greenville. The Mississippi Delta is home to many Greek families, and this dish was a favorite calling card of one of her new neighbors. It's a great make-ahead-and-freeze dish, which is exactly what Mary Lynn did. The creamy filling and flaky topping create a delicious flavor. Phyllo pastry might at first seem a bit intimidating to tackle, but after doing it once, you realize there's nothing to it!

In our cooking classes, young cooks and their parents never tire of making Big Fat Greek Pizza. The crust for this unique "pizza" is made by layering sheets of phyllo in a baking pan and topping it with layers of tasty ingredients. Our mix-and-match menu features a salad and a variety of main courses from which to choose.

We made pastitsio with Martha Stewart on her show *MARTHA*. Appearing with her was a dream come true for both of us, and we headed to New York with families in tow. Cooking on national television isn't really so different from cooking for a busy family: There's only a small window of time, so you have to be prepared and work quickly. Martha asked what we like about this recipe, and we told her that it covers all of the food groups and can be made ahead—not to mention that the pastitsio and Tossed Greek Salad Bowl make a delicious dinner!

Big Fat Greek Pizza

½ cup butter, melted

¼ cup plus 2 tablespoons olive oil

1 cup finely chopped onions

3 large cloves garlic, crushed

¼ teaspoon salt

½ teaspoon dried basil, crushed

½ teaspoon dried oregano

Juice of ½ large lemon

Freshly ground black pepper, to taste

1 pound fresh spinach, cleaned, stemmed, and chopped, or 1 10-ounce package frozen chopped spinach

1 package phyllo pastry dough

1½ cups crumbled feta or farmer's cheese

4 cups (1 pound) shredded mozzarella cheese

4 Roma tomatoes, thinly sliced

¾ cup fine bread crumbs

Preheat oven to 400°. Butter a large baking tray. Also, combine butter with ¼ cup oil. Set aside.

In a large skillet, cook onions and garlic with salt in remaining 2 tablespoons oil, until onions are translucent and soft. Add basil, oregano, lemon juice, pepper, and spinach and cook over fairly high heat, stirring until spinach is limp and liquid is evaporated.

On buttered baking tray, begin layering sheets of phyllo, brushing each surface with a generous amount of combined butter and olive oil. Continue layering sheets until you have used them all. Brush top surface of the stack with remaining butter/olive oil mixture.

Use a slotted spoon to transfer spinach mixture from skillet to pastry stack, leaving behind whatever liquid failed to evaporate. Spread spinach mixture evenly in place, leaving a ½-inch border of pastry.

Sprinkle with feta or farmer's cheese, plus half the mozzarella.

Dredge tomato slices in bread crumbs, arrange these on top of the pizza, and toss remaining mozzarella over tomatoes.

Bake uncovered for 20–25 minutes.

Yield: 8 servings

Kitchen Notes

- To remove moisture from spinach, place in a colander in the sink and squeeze spinach into a ball. Use paper towels to remove excess moisture.

- This also works well as an appetizer.

Pastitsio with Pizzazz!

1 tablespoon olive oil

1 medium onion, finely chopped

2 garlic cloves, pressed

1 pound lean ground beef

2 14.5-ounce cans diced tomatoes, drained

2 teaspoons dried oregano

1½ teaspoons cinnamon

1¾ teaspoons salt

¼ teaspoon freshly ground black pepper

8 ounces elbow macaroni

3 tablespoons butter

⅓ cup all-purpose flour

1 quart whole milk

2 large eggs

1 cup (4 ounces) freshly grated Parmesan cheese

1 cup (4 ounces) crumbled feta cheese

Preheat oven to 375°.

Heat oil in a large skillet over medium heat. Add onion and garlic and cook, stirring occasionally, until onion is translucent, 7 minutes.

Stir in beef and cook, breaking up meat with the back of a spoon, until browned, about 7 minutes. Spoon off all but 1 tablespoon fat.

Stir in tomatoes, oregano, cinnamon, 1 teaspoon salt, and pepper.

Bring to a boil, then reduce heat to low, cover, and simmer for 15 minutes. Uncover and simmer for 15 minutes more.

Meanwhile, cook macaroni according to package directions. Drain.

Melt butter in a large saucepan over medium heat. Whisk in flour for 1 minute.

Increase heat to high. Whisking constantly, add milk and remaining ¾ teaspoon salt. Bring to a boil and remove from heat.

In a small bowl, beat eggs using a whisk. Beat 1 cup of hot cream-sauce mixture into eggs, then beat egg mixture into cream sauce. Whisk in ¾ cup Parmesan.

Grease a shallow 9- by 13-inch baking dish.

Transfer half of the macaroni to baking dish. Layer with 1½ cups cheese sauce. Spread beef mixture evenly over cheese sauce. Layer with remaining macaroni, then sprinkle with feta. Top with remaining cheese sauce and sprinkle with remaining ¼ cup Parmesan.

Bake until golden and bubbling, 35 minutes. Let stand until firm.

Yield: 8 servings

Mom's Marvelous Chicken Phyllo

6 boneless, skinless chicken breasts

White sauce (recipe below)

8 ounces cream cheese, softened

1 bunch green onions (tops and all), chopped

1 cup chopped celery

Salt and black pepper, to taste

1 teaspoon seafood seasoning

¼ cup dry cooking sherry

1 package phyllo pastry dough

½ cup butter, melted

WHITE SAUCE:

¾ cup butter

¾ cup all-purpose flour

1½ cups milk

1½ cups chicken broth

Salt and black pepper, to taste

Preheat oven to 350°.

Grease a 9- by 13-inch casserole dish.

Gently boil chicken for 20 minutes in a stockpot filled with water seasoned with salt and pepper. Allow chicken to cool, then cut into bite-size pieces. Save 1½ cups chicken broth for the white sauce.

Meanwhile, make white sauce by melting ¾ cup butter in a large saucepan. Add flour and stir with a whisk until thickened. Slowly add milk and broth, constantly stirring with whisk until completely blended. Cook over medium heat until a thick sauce is made.

Add cream cheese to white sauce. Stir in onions, celery, and chicken. Blend well.

Mix in salt, pepper, seafood seasoning, and sherry.

Place in casserole dish.

Layer 1 sheet of phyllo dough on top of chicken mixture in casserole dish. Brush generously with butter, then add another sheet. Repeat until there are 11 layers.

Bake for 40–45 minutes, or until top is light brown and filling is bubbly.

Allow to set for 5–10 minutes before cutting. Serve.

Yield: 8 servings

Kitchen Note

- While working with phyllo dough, keep it covered with a damp towel and take out one sheet at a time.

Tossed Greek Salad Bowl

SALAD:

1 head romaine lettuce, washed, dried, and torn into bite-size pieces

½ head iceberg lettuce, washed, dried, and torn into bite-size pieces

12 cherry tomatoes

1 cup crumbled feta cheese

½ small red onion, chopped

1 cucumber, peeled and chopped, seeds removed

12 kalamata olives, pitted and cut in half

6 pepperoncini peppers

DRESSING:

6 tablespoons olive oil

4 tablespoons fresh lemon juice

2 teaspoons minced garlic

1 teaspoon dried oregano

1 2-ounce can anchovies, mashed

½ teaspoon salt, or to taste

½ teaspoon black pepper, or to taste

½ teaspoon sugar

In a large bowl, layer salad ingredients in the order given.

Place dressing ingredients into a blender and pulse until combined.

When ready to serve salad, pour dressing over layered ingredients and toss.

Yield: 8 servings

Kitchen Notes

- Dressing can be made ahead, and leftover dressing can be refrigerated up to 1 week.

- Layer the salad ahead of time, cover with plastic wrap, and refrigerate. Add the dressing when ready to serve.

Feta Pita Toast

2 tablespoons butter

½ cup chopped onion

2 cups (8 ounces) crumbled feta cheese

1 teaspoon lemon juice

½ teaspoon Greek seasoning

Pinch of cayenne pepper

6 pitas

½ cup (2 ounces) grated Parmesan cheese

Melt butter in a medium skillet. Add onion and sauté for 2–3 minutes over medium heat.

Remove from heat and add feta, lemon juice, Greek seasoning, and pepper.

Preheat oven to 400°.

Line a baking sheet with parchment paper.

Cut pitas in half, then cut the halves in half to make 4 wedges. Then make the 4 wedges into 8 wedges by cutting apart.

Place 1 heaping tablespoon feta mixture on each wedge, then place on baking sheet.

Sprinkle with Parmesan.

Bake for 10–12 minutes, or until cheeses are slightly melted and hot. Serve.

Yield: 8 servings

Kitchen Notes

- With a table knife, cut pita into triangles, like cutting a pie.
- This is a great make-ahead party recipe and can be heated as guests arrive.

The Very Best Baklava

1 package phyllo pastry, thawed

½ cup butter, melted

FILLING:

¾ cup light brown sugar

½ teaspoon cinnamon

¼ teaspoon allspice

¼ cup butter, melted

2 cups pecans or walnuts, finely chopped

Preheat oven to 350°.

Make filling by mixing the ingredients with a fork in a medium bowl. Set aside.

Keep phyllo covered with a slightly damp towel and work with 1 sheet at a time.

Place 1 sheet of phyllo on the work surface and brush entire sheet with butter. Repeat until you have 6 layers.

Cut buttered sheets into 2- by 14-inch strips.

Place a heaping teaspoon of filling on one end of a strip.

Fold the bottom left corner over to the right side. Then fold the bottom right corner over to the left side. Continue folding flag-fashion until the entire strip is folded into a triangle. Repeat the above steps using remaining sheets of phyllo.

Again, brush flags with butter.

Place on baking sheet. Bake for 15–20 minutes, or until golden brown.

Yield: about 3 dozen

Kitchen Notes

- Filling can be made the day before.
- Use a pastry brush.
- Scissors are handy for cutting phyllo into strips.
- Fold the baklava as you would fold a flag.

Sleepover
Party!

Asleepover party conjures up visions of late-night fun and frivolity for kids, and this menu offers a creative alternative to the incessant chatter of television and drone of video games. With five children between us and dozens of their friends in and out of our homes for weekend sleepovers, we can testify without hesitation that these recipes are "tried and true."

Because of the magic these worked in our own kitchens, this menu became the theme of one of our most requested classes. Many a parent has stopped one of us in the market or car-pool line to extol the virtues of letting kids take over the kitchen on a sleepover night. We teach Sleepover Party cooking classes on Saturday mornings and invite the kids to come in their pajamas. It makes the class even more fun and special. Parents are always on the lookout for a new, different, and engaging birthday party theme, and this class makes a delightful party. We've seen some darling invitations inviting sleepyheads to come to a Saturday morning cooking class in their pj's. We've now taught almost a hundred Sleepover Party classes, and with a completely kid-friendly menu, parents never fail to be "wowed" by the cute, creative, and balanced food items the kids prepare.

To get your own party started, begin with the ever-requested All-Night Nacho Dip. This is one of our all-time favorites, and it's not just for kids! You can make it in 5 minutes, so it's also the perfect quick treat when you have to take a snack to a party or school function. We've seen it dressed up and presented at the finest of parties. For Creatures in a Blanket, the kids build the creatures bit by bit and are delighted when they see the final products. Caramel popcorn is one of our children's favorites, and we're called on to make it whenever there is a school trip. We break it into pieces and place it in individual plastic storage bags to distribute to everyone on the school bus. Pajama Peanut-Butter Balls are a no-cook treat that everybody loves, especially washed down with Didn't-Sleep-a-Wink Pink Drink. This funny food will captivate even the finickiest of eaters.

Creatures in a Blanket

2 8-ounce cans crescent dinner rolls

8 1-ounce slices cooked ham or turkey

8 single slices Swiss or Cheddar cheese

16 frozen breaded wing-shaped chicken patties, slightly thawed

Squirt bottles of mustard and red, green, or blue ketchup

Preheat oven to 375°.

Line a baking sheet with parchment paper.

Separate dough into eight 4- by 7½-inch rectangles and firmly press perforations to seal.

For each sandwich, place one rectangle on sheet pan.

Top with 1 slice meat at one end of dough. Place 1 slice cheese on top.

Place 2 chicken patties, side by side, on meat and cheese.

Fold ⅔ of the dough over chicken from bottom up, leaving about 1½ inches of chicken uncovered, for the creatures' heads. Press sides of sandwich with fork to seal edges.

Bake at 375° for 10–12 minutes, or until crust is golden brown and chicken is hot.

Make faces and hair with mustard and ketchup. Mustard is great for hair, red ketchup is great for mouths, and green or blue ketchup is great for eyes.

Yield: 8 servings

Kitchen Notes

- Parchment paper is handy for this recipe. Write the name of the person who made each "creature" on the paper so once the sandwiches are cooked, each child can decorate his or her own. Also, there is no messy, sticky cleanup for the pan.

- One can of refrigerated crescent rolls makes four creatures.

Pajama Peanut-Butter Balls

1 cup peanut butter, creamy or crunchy

1 cup light corn syrup

1¼ cups powdered milk

1¼ cups confectioners' sugar plus more for rolling

Place peanut butter, corn syrup, powdered milk, and confectioners' sugar in a mixing bowl and stir until thoroughly combined.

Using your hands, roll mixture into as many small, bite-size balls as possible.

Place extra confectioners' sugar in a shallow pie tin or plate and roll balls in sugar to coat.

Eat and enjoy.

Yield: 24 balls, depending on size

Kitchen Notes

- This is a simple no-bake recipe.

- It's easier to roll dough into balls using fingertips instead of your whole hand.

- If the dough becomes too sticky, roll the balls in extra confectioners' sugar.

All-Night Nacho Dip

2 8-ounce packages cream cheese

1 15-ounce can chili (no beans)

2 cups (8 ounces) shredded Monterey Jack cheese, or a mixture of Monterey Jack and Cheddar

Tortilla chips

Using a spatula, spread cream cheese in 1 layer along the bottom of your most festive 8- by 8-inch baking dish.

Top with chili and use a spoon to spread evenly over cream cheese.

Sprinkle shredded cheese evenly over chili.

Bake at 350° for 10-12 minutes or microwave for about 4 minutes, or until melted.

Enjoy with tortilla chips.

Yield: about 3 cups

Kitchen Note

- Use our recipe as a guide, and then add your own favorite ingredients such as black olives, jalapeño or green chile peppers, salsa, or green onion.

No-Curfew Caramel Popcorn

1 cup sugar

½ cup butter

½ cup light corn syrup

1 teaspoon salt

½ teaspoon baking soda

1 teaspoon vanilla extract

2 3-ounce packages microwave popcorn, popped (16 cups)

Preheat oven to 250°.

Lightly grease 2 shallow roasting pans.

In a saucepan, stir together sugar, butter, corn syrup, and salt.

Bring to a boil over medium heat, stirring constantly.

Remove mixture from heat and stir in baking soda and vanilla extract.

Place half of popcorn in each pan. Pour sugar mixture evenly over popcorn, then stir well with a lightly greased spatula.

Bake at 250° for 1 hour, stirring every 15 minutes. Spread on waxed paper to cool, breaking apart large clumps as mixture cools.

Store in airtight containers.

Yield: 16 cups

Kitchen Notes

- Caramel popcorn makes a great holiday gift! Place in cellophane bags and tie with colorful ribbon.

- For a different flavor, add salted pecans, almonds, or peanuts.

Didn't-Sleep-a-Wink Pink Drink

2 cups low-fat frozen vanilla yogurt

1 cup frozen sweetened strawberries, partially thawed

2 cups low-fat milk

8 cherries, for garnish

Working in batches, combine yogurt, strawberries, and milk in a blender and whirl until smooth.

Pour equal amounts into 8 glasses.

Add a cherry to each glass and serve.

Yield: 8 servings

Kitchen Notes

- Use your favorite fruit along with your favorite frozen yogurt to customize your smoothie.

- If consistency seems too thick for your taste, simply thin with a bit more milk.

Backyard Burger Bash

Rob's Grilled Cheddar Burgers

Katie's Homemade Potato Chips

Paint Magic

Slow-Cooked BBQ Baked Beans

The Perfect Peach-Blueberry Cobbler

Backyard Brown-Sugar Brownies

Backyard burgers are a traditional American family favorite, and our families are no exception. Living in the Deep South, we can find an excuse to cook outside nearly every month of the year. Even in deepest winter, we can still be found shivering over the outdoor grill in quest of the perfect burger.

Making hamburger patties, peeling potatoes, and measuring for brownies are fun jobs for the younger kids, while slicing and grilling chores are reserved for older kids or adults. Rob, Leslie's teenage son, is such an accomplished backyard cook that our Grilled Cheddar Burgers bear his name. We've added a quirky ingredient—pickle juice—to moisten the ground chuck and add extra flavor, yet it almost seems an obvious choice. My niece Katie has been assisting in our cooking classes since she was 12. When she heard we were looking for a recipe for homemade chips, she claimed that she had the *best*. And after trying Katie's Homemade Potato Chips, I think you'll agree. Fresh peach-blueberry cobbler is an incomparable summer treat and easy to make, with no crust required. In my home, this cobbler is on the menu whenever peaches and blueberries are in season, whether I'm entertaining on paper plates in the backyard or on fine china at the dining room table. I place the cobbler in the oven as my guests arrive, and the timing is perfect. I pull it out of the oven when it's time for dessert, add a dollop of ice cream, and serve immediately.

The slow-cooked baked beans have always been my mother's favorite dish to take to a cookout. I remember as a child helping her cut the bacon and chop the onions the day before. She would put the beans in a cast-iron pot on the stove the morning of the cookout and let them simmer. I remember the wonderful aroma and peeking in the pot to watch them cook down. I recently asked her why this was always her dish of choice for an outdoor event, and her answer was that men love this. With a house full of four boys and my dad, she knew what she was talking about.

Rob's Grilled Cheddar Burgers

2 pounds ground chuck (20 percent fat is ideal)

2 tablespoons dill pickle juice

2 tablespoons Montreal Steak Seasoning

8 slices Cheddar cheese

8 hamburger buns

In a medium bowl, combine ground chuck, pickle juice, and steak seasoning and mix well.

Make into patties of 1-inch thickness.

Make sure the grill is good and hot.

Grill over a hot fire, flipping once, for about 4–5 minutes per side for medium doneness. Add cheese after flipping.

If you are not using a grill to cook the burgers, then heat a large nonstick skillet over medium-high heat until hot.

Add patties and cook about 4–5 minutes per side, turning once.

Remove patties from skillet and cover to keep warm.

Serve on buns, perhaps topped with ketchup, mustard, or chili sauce.

Yield: 8 large or 10 medium patties

Kitchen Note

● Make hamburger patties ahead of time. Cover and refrigerate until ready to grill.

Rob's Grilled Cheddar Burgers (opposite) and Katie's Homemade Potato Chips with Paint Magic (page 116)

Katie's Homemade Potato Chips

4 medium potatoes

Paint Magic (see below)

Preheat oven to 350°.

Wash potatoes and cut in slices or long strips, skin on.

Place in a single layer on a baking pan covered with aluminum foil or parchment. (We prefer parchment because aluminum foil tends to stick.)

Brush with Paint Magic until well coated.

Bake for 20 minutes.

Turn and brush again with Paint Magic.

Bake for 45–50 minutes, or until brown.

Yield: 6–8 servings

Kitchen Notes

- Line your pan with foil or parchment for easier cleanup.

- Place potato strips in a bowl of ice water with ¼ cup white vinegar and soak for 10 minutes before baking. Drain in colander. This will make them extracrisp!

- The blue cheese dressing on page 27 is an excellent accompaniment for these chips.

Paint Magic

½ cup olive oil

¼ cup fresh lemon juice

¼ cup Worcestershire sauce

Up to 5 garlic cloves

½ teaspoon black pepper

Mix all ingredients in a blender until smooth.

Pour into a container with a top.

Store in the refrigerator for up to 1 week.

When ready to use, brush it on vegetables or meat before and during cooking.

May also be used as a dip, marinade, or sauce for meats and vegetables.

Yield: 1 cup

Slow-Cooked BBQ Baked Beans

¼ pound bacon strips, cut into thirds

1 medium onion, finely chopped

3 14.5-ounce cans pork and beans

½ cup ketchup

1 cup light brown sugar, lightly packed

2 tablespoons yellow mustard

2 tablespoons Worcestershire sauce

3 shakes Tabasco sauce

Cook bacon in a 4-quart pot until crisp. Drain all but 2 tablespoons grease.

Add onion and sauté until clear.

Add beans and stir.

Add remaining ingredients.

Stir well and simmer, uncovered, until cooked down to desired consistency (about 2 hours).

Yield: 6–8 servings

Kitchen Note

- Plan ahead. Chop the bacon and onions the day before.

The Perfect Peach-Blueberry Cobbler

4–5 large peaches, peeled and sliced

3 tablespoons unsalted butter

1 tablespoon lemon juice

⅓ cup sugar

1 cup fresh blueberries

5 tablespoons unsalted butter

1 cup all-purpose flour

⅔ cup sugar

½ teaspoon salt

1½ teaspoons baking powder

1 cup heavy cream

1 egg yolk

Vanilla ice cream

TO PREPARE FRUIT:

Cut peaches into bite-size pieces.

Heat butter in a large skillet.

Add peaches, lemon juice, and sugar.

Cook over medium heat until softened, 2–3 minutes.

Gently toss in blueberries.

TO MAKE TOPPING:

Preheat oven to 350°. Place butter in a 9-inch square pan and put in oven to melt.

Combine flour, sugar, salt, and baking powder in a mixing bowl.

Add cream and egg yolk and mix well.

Remove baking pan from oven and stir butter into batter, leaving just enough to coat the pan.

Spoon peaches and blueberries into pan and pour batter on top.

Place in oven.

Check after 25 minutes. If top is brown, cover loosely with foil.

Bake until a knife or wooden pick inserted near the middle comes out clean. This usually takes 30–35 minutes.

Cool.

Serve warm with vanilla ice cream.

Yield: 6–8 servings

Backyard Brown-Sugar Brownies

BROWNIES:

2 ounces unsweetened chocolate

1 cup all-purpose flour, sifted

¼ teaspoon salt

¾ teaspoon cinnamon

½ teaspoon baking soda

⅔ cup butter

1¼ cups light brown sugar, packed

1 large egg

1 teaspoon vanilla extract

⅓ cup sour cream

1 cup pecans (optional)

BUTTERY CINNAMON FROSTING:

1½ cups confectioners' sugar, sifted

¼ teaspoon cinnamon

Pinch of salt

3 tablespoons butter, softened

1 tablespoon milk

½ teaspoon vanilla extract

TO MAKE BROWNIES:

Preheat oven to 350°.

Grease and flour an 8- or 9-inch square brownie pan.

Melt chocolate in a double boiler. Cool.

Combine flour, salt, cinnamon, and baking soda. Sift and set aside.

In a large bowl, cream butter with an electric mixer.

Add brown sugar in thirds and continue to cream until fluffy.

Add egg and beat until smooth. Stir in vanilla extract, sour cream, and melted chocolate.

Fold in flour mixture. Stir in pecans, if desired.

Bake in center of oven 25–30 minutes, or until top is dry and wooden pick inserted 1 inch from center comes out barely moist. Depending on the oven, it may take longer than 30 minutes to cook completely.

Cool completely on a rack.

Sift confectioners' sugar, cinnamon, and salt.

With an electric mixer, cream butter. Add sifted ingredients. Mix well.

Add milk and vanilla extract. Beat until fluffy.

Spread on brownies. Cut into 2–3-inch squares.

Yield: 9–12 brownies

Kitchen Notes

- Chocolate should be heated slowly and gently in a double boiler. If you don't have a double boiler, make one by setting a heatproof bowl atop a saucepan filled with 2 to 3 inches of water.

- When measuring brown sugar, pack it tightly in a measuring cup.

- Make sure brownies are completely cool before frosting.

- When baking, remember to use exact measurements.

Pool Party

Annie's Sassy Salsa

Baked Chicken Nuggets on a Stick

Oven-Baked Corn-Dog Skewers

On- or Off-the-Grill Buttered Corn

Poolside Potato Salad

Summer Fruit Skewers with Caramel
or Orange-Cream Fruit Dip

Re Re's Sand Cookies

Scrumptious Bread Pudding with Fresh Berries

Make a splash with this perfect-for-pool-or-backyard-party menu. Almost everything can be done ahead of time, and that's a good thing because the pull of the pool commands the attention of even the best young kitchen helper. Enhancing the fun and frivolity of the pool experience is always my goal, and, in this instance, the food is secondary. I want to enjoy the fun and sun along with my children, so when I get to the poolside, my planning and preparation have long been completed.

When putting together an outdoor-party menu like this, I look for recipes that are easy to eat on the run. Grab-and-go foods like Baked Chicken Nuggets on a Stick or Oven-Baked Corn-Dog Skewers work well in settings where the playful atmosphere creates short attention spans at the table. My kids love all of these recipes—especially the bread pudding, a special treat that's baked with love by my Aunt Janet, who braves the splashing and squealing to spend time at the pool with my family.

Make it your goal, like mine, to stay in a lounge chair and out of the kitchen as much as possible. Corn can be shucked, buttered, and wrapped in advance. Re Re's Sand Cookies, one of my mom's tried-and-true summer recipes, can be made ahead. Prepare the potato salad without adding the mayonnaise, then cover and refrigerate. Stir in the mayo before heading out to the pool. Annie's Sassy Salsa is just as colorful and sassy as its namesake (my daughter) and can be premade, chilled, and ready for snacking. The chicken nuggets and corn-dog skewers can be prepared up to the point of baking.

And if you don't have an Aunt Janet to prepare the bread pudding, enjoy making this one the night before. Sitting overnight makes it even more scrumptious!

Annie's Sassy Salsa

2 15-ounce cans black beans, drained
  and rinsed

1 16-ounce can white corn, drained

½ cup finely chopped cilantro

¼ cup finely chopped green onions

⅓ cup fresh lime juice

3 tablespoons olive oil

1 tablespoon cumin

½–1 teaspoon salt, to taste

  Ground black pepper, to taste

1 4-ounce can chopped green chiles

4 dashes hot sauce (if desired)

Combine all ingredients in order given and mix well.

Refrigerate until ready to serve.

Serve with tortilla chips or Fritos Scoops! Corn Chips.

Yield: 6 cups

Kitchen Notes

- Drain and rinse the black beans in a colander in the sink.
- Use a lemon juicer for juicing the lime.

Baked Chicken Nuggets on a Stick

Wooden skewers

6 boneless, skinless chicken breasts

½ cup plain bread crumbs, either fresh or dry

¼ cup (1 ounce) grated Parmesan cheese

1 teaspoon garlic salt

½ cup butter, melted

Preheat oven to 400°.

Soak skewers in water for at least 20 minutes before using.

Line a baking sheet with foil.

Cut chicken into bite-size chunks.

Mix bread crumbs with cheese and garlic salt.

Dip chicken into butter.

Roll in crumb mixture.

Stick 3 chicken chunks on a skewer. Lay on foil-lined baking sheet.

Bake for 10–12 minutes.

Yield: 6–8 servings

Kitchen Note

● Use chicken tenders, if desired.

Oven-Baked Corn-Dog Skewers

Wooden skewers

3 tablespoons yellow cornmeal

1 11.5-ounce can refrigerated cornbread
twists or breadsticks

1 tablespoon yellow mustard

8 hot dogs

Preheat oven to 400°.

Soak skewers in water for at least 20 minutes before using.

Sprinkle cornmeal on a sheet of waxed paper.

Separate cornbread or breadstick dough into 8 long strips.

Unroll dough on cornmeal, then press into cornmeal.

Spread dough with mustard.

To make each corn dog, coil 1 dough strip around each hot dog.

For extra crunchiness, roll again in cornmeal.

Insert skewer lengthwise through hot dog, securing dough on each end.

Place corn dogs on a baking sheet lined with parchment paper.

Bake for 12–15 minutes, or until golden brown.

Yield: 8 servings

Oven-Baked Corn-Dog Skewers (opposite), and Poolside Potato Salad (page 129)

On- or Off-the-Grill Buttered Corn

8 ears corn

½ cup butter

8 12- by 8-inch squares aluminum foil

1 teaspoon Creole seasoning

Preheat oven to 350°.

Remove husks and silk from each ear of corn. Rinse corn and pat dry.

Cut butter into 8 equal pieces.

Set 1 ear of corn on top of each piece of foil. Place 1 butter pat on corn and sprinkle with some of the Creole seasoning.

Roll up foil over corn. Tuck in sides. Place corn on a baking sheet. Bake until tender, about 1 hour.

Remove baking sheet from oven and let cool for 5 minutes before taking corn out of hot foil.

Be careful unwrapping foil—both the steam and corn are hot!

You may also cook on a medium-fire grill for about 45 minutes, or until tender.

Yield: 8 servings

Kitchen Note

- For faster cooking while retaining good grilled taste, wrap the corn (husk and all) in a damp paper towel and microwave for 7 minutes. After the corn cools, shuck, wrap in foil, and put on the grill.

Poolside Potato Salad

2 pounds new red potatoes, cubed

1 cup finely chopped celery

½ cup grated onion

¼ cup fresh parsley

4 hard-boiled eggs, chopped

1½ cups mayonnaise

2 tablespoons white vinegar

1 teaspoon salt

¼ teaspoon black pepper

½ teaspoon Creole seasoning

8 bacon slices, cooked crisp and crumbled (optional)

Cook potatoes in lightly salted water until tender, about 20 minutes.

Drain in a colander and rinse with cold water.

When slightly cool, add celery, onion, parsley, and eggs. Mix mayonnaise and vinegar together. Fold mayonnaise mixture into potato mixture. Season with salt, pepper, and Creole seasoning.

Add bacon, if desired.

Refrigerate until completely chilled.

Yield: 6 servings

Kitchen Note

- For perfect hard-boiled eggs, place eggs in single layer in a saucepan and cover with warm water. Bring to a boil over high heat. When water comes to a boil, immediately reduce the heat to the lowest setting and set a timer for 14 minutes. After 14 minutes, remove the pan with the eggs from the stove top and place in the sink. Run cold water into saucepan until the entire pan feels cool. Hard-boiled eggs will keep in their shells in the refrigerator for up to 2 weeks.

Summer Fruit Skewers

straws

bite-size pieces of different fruits: strawberries, apple wedges, grapes, melon, pineapple, orange, kiwifruit

To make each kebab, pinch the end of a straw and push it through a piece of fruit.

Slide fruit to other end of straw. You'll need 6–8 pieces per skewer.

Add more fruit to fill skewer with a range of colors.

Individually cover each kebab with plastic.

Wrap and refrigerate until it's time to eat.

Caramel Fruit Dip

¼ cup sugar

¾ cup light brown sugar, packed

1 teaspoon vanilla extract

8 ounces cream cheese, softened

Fresh fruit for dipping

Put sugars, vanilla extract, and cream cheese in a blender or food processor and blend or process until smooth.

Serve with a colorful assortment of seasonal fruit, such as apple slices, pear slices, and strawberries.

Yield: 1½ cups

Orange-Cream Fruit Dip

8 ounces cream cheese, softened

7 ounces marshmallow crème

2 tablespoons fresh orange juice

Fresh fruit for dipping

In a food processor or blender, mix cream cheese, marshmallow crème, and orange juice. Chill until ready to serve.

Serve with fresh fruit.

Yield: 1 cup

Re Re's Sand Cookies

½ cup butter

½ cup shortening

1 cup sugar plus more for pressing

1 egg

2½ cups all-purpose flour

¾ teaspoon salt

½ teaspoon baking soda

½ teaspoon baking powder

1 teaspoon vanilla extract

½ teaspoon almond extract

2 tablespoons milk

Preheat oven to 350°.

Line a baking sheet with parchment paper.

Beat butter and shortening together.

Add 1 cup sugar gradually and beat until fluffy.

Keep beating and add egg. Combine flour, salt, baking soda, and baking powder, stirring with a whisk. Slowly add dry ingredients to butter-and-egg mixture.

Stir in extracts and milk and blend.

Drop by tablespoons on a baking sheet.

Dip glass with a 2–3-inch bottom into a bowl of water, then a bowl of sugar, and press each cookie flat, one by one, onto the baking sheet.

Bake for 12 minutes.

Yield: 24–30 cookies

Scrumptious Bread Pudding with Fresh Berries

BREAD PUDDING:

1 loaf of French bread (1-pound loaf; day old is best)

2 ounces white chocolate

2 cups heavy cream

1 cup milk

1½ teaspoons vanilla extract

7 egg yolks

½ cup sugar

2 pinches of salt

Melted butter to coat pan

WHITE CHOCOLATE GANACHE:

10 ounces white chocolate

¾ cup heavy cream

1 teaspoon vanilla extract or brandy

BERRY SAUCE:

1 pound frozen raspberries or mixed berries, defrosted and strained, with excess juice reserved

Juice of ½ lemon

2 tablespoons heavy cream

¼ cup sugar

Fresh berries (blueberries, raspberries, blackberries, and strawberries)

TO MAKE BREAD PUDDING:

Preheat oven to 350°.

Tear bread into large chunks and place in a bowl.

In a double boiler, melt chocolate. Add cream, milk, and ½ teaspoon vanilla extract. Whisk until combined. Continue to whisk occasionally. Cook until tiny bubbles form on the surface. Do not let this mixture come to a boil. Remove from heat and cool.

In a large mixing bowl, whisk egg yolks vigorously. Add sugar and continue to whisk till mixture has lightened in color. Stir in salt and remaining 1 teaspoon vanilla extract.

While whisking, slowly add cream mixture to egg mixture.

Pour over bread and let sit for 5 minutes. Toss with hands to ensure that all bread has been coated.

Coat a 9- by 13-inch pan with melted butter and pour mixture into pan.

Place a sheet of parchment paper over pan and bake for 30 minutes. Remove paper and bake for another 10 minutes. While bread pudding is baking, prepare the ganache and sauce.

TO MAKE WHITE CHOCOLATE GANACHE:

Chop chocolate and place in a medium-size mixing bowl.

In a saucepan, heat cream and vanilla extract or brandy over medium heat until small bubbles begin to form. Do not bring mixture to a boil.

Remove cream mixture from heat and immediately pour over chocolate. Let stand for 5 minutes so that chocolate melts.

After 5 minutes, stir ganache until all chocolate is melted.

If you are making ganache in advance and keeping it in the refrigerator, make sure to microwave it for about 30 seconds before pouring it over the bread pudding.

TO MAKE BERRY SAUCE:

Drain defrosted berries and set aside juice.

Place berries in a blender or food processor and blend with lemon juice, cream, and sugar.

Strain well, making sure no seeds are left. If sauce looks too thick, simply add some of the reserved juice to thin it out.

The sauce should taste somewhat tart in order to complement the sweetness of the ganache.

TO FINISH BREAD PUDDING:

Serve with warmed white chocolate ganache and berry sauce. Garnish with fresh berries. A real treat!

Yield: 8–10 servings

Kitchen Notes

- A favorite technique is to put chocolate and berry sauces into squirt bottles and drizzle over the bread pudding or create designs on the serving plate.

- With leftover chocolate and berry sauces, create an entirely new dessert by drizzling either or both over vanilla ice cream.

Pizza
Parlor!

Perfect Pizza Crust

Best BBQ Chicken Pizza!

Farm Fresh Pizza

Design Your Own! Pizza

It-Only-Takes-a-Minute Pizza

Everyone Loves Cookie Pizza!

All-American Green Apple Pizza

Forget about the pizza deliveryman. You can deliver delicious dinners and family fun using ingredients and leftovers from your own refrigerator. Family members of all ages take pride in creating their own personal pizzas.

In our homes, pizza is a favorite meal anytime of the day—including breakfast. Design Your Own! pizzas have long been a favorite activity for Helen and her son, Martin. As small children, he and his neighborhood friends were fascinated with watching the yeast bubble and the dough rise. They loved "patting" the dough into round disks and adding the toppings all by themselves. Helen likes to turn the pizza making into even more of a party by putting ingredients and toppings in small bowls on the kitchen counter so each adult and child can easily create his or her own personal pizza.

My family enjoys eating breakfast foods on Sunday evenings, and Farm Fresh Pizza is a favorite. The boys cook the bacon and sausage and scramble the eggs, and Annie and I make the crust. On fall nights after football games, I serve pizza to the house full of hungry teenagers who always seem to find their way to my kitchen. The barbecue chicken pizza never fails to be a hit with the boys. Once it's out, it's gone. There are never any leftovers on this one. Another recipe I automatically turn to when autumn leaves are changing is our All-American Green Apple pizza. It conjures up thoughts of fall festivals and carnivals with crunchy apples and caramel. Dessert pizzas add a surprise element to any party or family night supper, and this one is scrumptious.

Once you master the perfect pizza crust, you'll see how easy it is to create a delicious meal or whip up a popular party appetizer in a matter of minutes with ingredients you have on hand. The key is always keeping a supply of yeast in the pantry.

Perfect Pizza Crust

1 package active dry yeast	1 teaspoon salt
1¼ cups lukewarm water	3 tablespoons extra-virgin olive oil
1 tablespoon honey	½ cup bread flour, for kneading
3½ cups all-purpose flour	

In a large bowl, combine yeast, water, and honey. Set aside until foamy, about 10 minutes.

Mix together all-purpose flour and salt. Add oil to mixture.

Slowly add yeast mixture to flour-and-salt mixture, using a wooden spoon. Stir to combine, making sure to incorporate all ingredients.

Transfer dough to a surface sprinkled with bread flour.

Knead dough and add remaining bread flour until dough is smooth and elastic, 5–7 minutes.

Cover dough with a clean dish towel and set aside to rise in a warm, draft-free place until doubled in size, about 1½ hours.

Punch down dough. On a lightly floured surface, using a floured rolling pin, roll dough into a circle the size of your pizza pan. Place in pizza pan coated with nonstick cooking spray. Add toppings of your choice and bake in a 400° oven for directed time.

Yield: Crust for 8-serving pizza

Kitchen Notes

- When adding water to the yeast and honey, it should be warm like a baby's bath, not hot.

- Once the yeast mixture foams and bubbles, it's ready for the flour. If there are no bubbles, throw it out and start with a new package of yeast.

- On a lightly floured surface, knead the dough by pressing it away from you with the heel of your hand and folding it over and over until smooth and elastic. It helps to grease your hands with a little olive oil to prevent sticking.

- Give the dough a few good punches with your fist, then use a lightly floured rolling pin and roll the dough out to fit your pizza pan.

- Make the crust thick or thin, whichever you prefer.

Best BBQ Chicken Pizza!

2 pounds chicken

½ cup barbecue sauce

1½ teaspoons olive oil

Perfect Pizza Crust (opposite page)

1 cup (4 ounces) shredded mozzarella cheese

½ cup (2 ounces) shredded smoked Gouda cheese

½ cup sliced red onion

2 teaspoons finely chopped fresh cilantro

Cut chicken into bite-size cubes and marinate in ¼ cup barbecue sauce in the refrigerator for at least 2 hours.

Preheat oven to 400°.

Heat oil in a small frying pan on your stove top. Sauté chicken in pan for 4–5 minutes, or until tender.

Pat out crust onto a 9- by 13-inch baking sheet or pizza pan and spread evenly with remaining ¼ cup barbecue sauce.

Sprinkle ½ cup mozzarella and all of the Gouda over the sauce.

Place chicken and onion on top.

Sprinkle remaining ½ cup mozzarella around center of pizza.

Cilantro goes on top of the mozzarella.

Bake pizza for 10–12 minutes, or until crust is light brown.

When pizza is done, remove from oven and make 4 even cuts across the pie. This will give you 8 slices.

Yield: 8 servings

Kitchen Notes

- A time-saver is to buy a cooked whole rotisserie chicken at the market and add barbecue sauce.
- To serve as an appetizer, make in a rectangular pan and cut into squares.

Farm Fresh Pizza

CRUST:

2 cups all-purpose flour

1½ teaspoons baking powder

1 teaspoon sugar

½ teaspoon salt

¼ cup butter, cut into small pieces

¾ cup grated Cheddar cheese

¾ cup milk

TOPPING:

1 16-ounce tube sausage, browned, drained, and crumbled, or 1 pound bacon, cooked and crumbled

1 tablespoon butter

8 large eggs, lightly beaten

Salt and black pepper, to taste

1½ cups grated Cheddar cheese

TO MAKE CRUST:

Sift flour, baking powder, sugar, and salt into a large mixing bowl.

Using a pastry blender or your fingers, cut or rub butter into dry ingredients until it is broken into very small pieces.

Add ¾ cup cheese and toss lightly. Make a well in dry ingredients, then add milk. Stir gently, just until dough is mixed, then let it sit for several minutes.

Preheat oven to 400°.

Butter a 12-inch round pizza pan.

Dust dough and your hands with flour, then place dough in middle of pan and press it into a circle, touching edge of pan. Pinch edge into a slightly raised rim.

Bake for 12–15 minutes, or until top of crust is a light golden brown.

TO MAKE TOPPING:

Brown sausage or bacon in a skillet over medium heat. Remove with a slotted spoon and drain on a paper towel.

Using a large skillet, melt butter over medium-low heat.

Add eggs and scramble lightly, adding salt and pepper. Immediately remove eggs from heat.

Spoon eggs over baked crust, spreading them with a fork. Top with sausage or bacon and cheese. Return pan to oven and bake 5 minutes longer, or until cheese has melted. Slice and serve right away.

Yield: 6–8 servings

Design Your Own! Pizza

1 refrigerated canned pizza crust

Pizza sauce, as needed

Choice of toppings: pepperoni, Canadian bacon, cooked and crumbled bacon, browned hamburger meat; broccoli, mushrooms, fresh basil, roasted red bell peppers, black olives; Parmesan, mozzarella, and/or Cheddar cheese

Preheat oven to 400°.

Open can of crust and press into pizza pan. Bake for 5 minutes. Remove from oven.

Spread sauce on crust.

Design with your favorite toppings. Bake for 10–12 minutes, or until brown. Enjoy!

Yield: 8 servings

It-Only-Takes-a-Minute Pizza

1 16.3-ounce can refrigerated big biscuits

1 cup pizza sauce, store-bought

1½ cups grated mozzarella cheese

Choice of toppings: pepperoni, Canadian bacon, mushrooms, black olives

Preheat oven to 400°.

Open can of biscuits and have the children flatten biscuits into disks by patting dough between their hands.

Place flattened disks on a baking sheet that has been coated with nonstick cooking spray or lined with parchment paper. Spread sauce and cheese over each.

Allow children to "decorate" their individual little pizzas with their favorite toppings.

Bake for 10–12 minutes, or until brown.

Enjoy!

Yield: 8 servings

Everyone Loves Cookie Pizza!

COOKIE CRUST:

2 eggs

1 cup light brown sugar, packed

½ cup granulated sugar

1 cup butter, softened

2 teaspoons vanilla extract

2½ cups all-purpose flour

1 teaspoon baking soda

CHOCOLATE PIZZA SAUCE:

4 tablespoons butter, softened

3 cups confectioners' sugar, sifted

3 tablespoons cocoa powder, sifted

4 tablespoons milk

1 teaspoon vanilla extract

Pinch of salt

TOPPINGS:

Choose from these suggested candies: multicolored sprinkles, colored sugar, mini chocolate chips, gummy worms, silver balls, mini marshmallows, M&Ms

Preheat oven to 350°. Coat a pizza pan with nonstick cooking spray.

TO MAKE COOKIE CRUST:

Mix eggs, sugars, butter, and vanilla extract together. Stir with a wooden spoon until mixed.

Add flour and baking soda to sugar mixture.

Spread or pat dough into pizza pan, using back of spoon or a piece of waxed paper pressed with your hand (flouring hands helps).

Bake for about 15-20 minutes, or until crust is golden brown. Allow to cool.

While crust is cooling, make chocolate pizza sauce.

TO MAKE CHOCOLATE PIZZA SAUCE:

In a large mixing bowl, cream butter, confectioners' sugar, and cocoa. Add milk, vanilla extract, and salt and beat until smooth. Spread on cooled crust. This sauce will keep in a covered container in the refrigerator for about 1 week.

Right away, sprinkle with candies, adding others if you like.

Yield: 16 servings

All-American Green Apple Pizza

2 cups all-purpose flour

2 cups quick-cooking oats

1½ cups light brown sugar, packed

1 teaspoon baking soda

1¼ cups margarine or butter, melted

1½ cups caramel ice cream topping

½ cup all-purpose flour

2 cups peeled and coarsely chopped Granny Smith apples

Heat oven to 350°.

Grease a 15- by 10- by 1-inch baking pan or round pizza pan.

In a large bowl, combine flour, oats, sugar, baking soda, and margarine or butter and mix until crumbly.

Press half of mixture (about 2½ cups) in bottom of pan to form base.

Reserve remaining mixture for topping. Bake at 350° for 8 minutes.

Meanwhile, in small saucepan, combine caramel topping and flour and blend well.

Bring to a boil over medium heat, stirring constantly. Boil 3–5 minutes, or until mixture thickens slightly, stirring constantly.

Remove pan from oven. Sprinkle apples over warm crust. Pour caramel mixture evenly over top. Sprinkle with reserved topping mixture.

Return pan to oven and bake for an additional 25–30 minutes, or until golden brown. Cool at room temperature for 30 minutes.

Refrigerate for 30 minutes or until set.

Cut into slices.

Yield: 8 servings

Kitchen Notes

- Do not substitute red apples.
- Serve with vanilla ice cream—it's as good as homemade apple pie.

Soup by the Spoonfuls

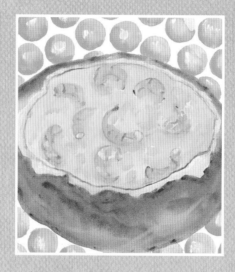

Phillip's Cheese Soup

Cozy Cream-of-Tomato Soup

Roll-Over-and-Play-Sick Soup

Flavorful Tortilla Soup

Simple Shrimp Chowder

Hearty Chili

There is nothing like a loving spoonful of soup to make us feel warm, secure, and nourished. When we teach the children in our classes to make soup, we know we are helping them create memories that will last a lifetime. Making soup is a rewarding group experience, whether in a cooking class or in the family kitchen. Roll-Over-and-Play-Sick Soup is a vegetable soup handed down from my mother-in-law, Marsh, and served when anyone in the family is sick. Hearty Chili was passed along by Helen's younger brother, Todd, who made this soup for his children's entire elementary school, and there wasn't a drop left in the pot.

Soup is a year-round favorite at my house. There's nothing I enjoy more than getting out a big pot and making soup. The different textures and flavors appeal to me as a cook, and as a mother, I feel I am nourishing my family when I serve them one of my soups. Setting a table for a soup supper is another pleasure. I discovered long ago that soup bowls don't have to be round and boring, so I'm always on the lookout for a fanciful container or unusual bowl for serving my creations. I put out a variety of toppings so everyone at the table can personalize their soup. Sometimes I offer a variety of cheeses or different herbs to vary the flavor. Crème fraîche or sour cream enhances most any soup.

Stirring a soup pot stirs something in my soul and brings warmth and joy to the family table. My hope as a mom and as a cook is that years from now, my children will stir a pot of soup in their own kitchens and think of me.

Phillip's Cheese Soup

4 tablespoons butter

½ cup finely chopped carrots

½ cup finely chopped green pepper

½ cup finely chopped onion

½ cup finely chopped celery

½ cup all-purpose flour

3 cans chicken broth

3 cups (12 ounces) shredded Cheddar cheese

4 cups milk

Salt and white pepper, to taste

In a soup pot, melt butter. Add vegetables and simmer until tender but not browned. Whisk in flour and cook, stirring, for 1 minute.

Add broth and cook, stirring, until thickened. Turn heat to low.

Add cheese and cook, stirring, until melted.

Stir in milk and bring to a simmer. Season to taste.

Yield: 8 servings

Cozy Cream-of-Tomato Soup

1 large onion, finely chopped

3 tablespoons olive oil

1 28-ounce can crushed tomatoes, undrained

2 cups tomato juice

1 cup heavy cream

½ teaspoon salt

¼ teaspoon black pepper

In a soup pot over medium heat, sauté onion in oil until tender, about 4–5 minutes.

Add tomatoes and tomato juice.

Simmer for 25 minutes.

Add cream, salt, and pepper.

Gently heat through. Serve warm.

Yield: 8 servings

Roll-Over-and-Play-Sick Soup

2 pounds round steak, cut into bite-size pieces

2 medium onions, chopped

1 tablespoon olive oil

1½ cups chopped celery

6 medium carrots, peeled and sliced

1 10-ounce package frozen sliced okra

1 10-ounce package frozen baby lima beans

1 10-ounce package frozen corn

3 14.5-ounce cans beef broth

2 cans Rotel tomatoes

2 bay leaves

1 teaspoon salt

1 teaspoon black pepper

2 teaspoons spicy spaghetti seasoning or Italian seasoning

1 teaspoon Creole seasoning

1 tablespoon soy sauce

In a large Dutch oven, cook steak and onions in oil until meat is brown, about 5–7 minutes.

Add celery, carrots, okra, lima beans, corn, broth, and tomatoes. Mix well to distribute ingredients.

Stir in bay leaves, salt, pepper, spaghetti or Italian seasoning, Creole seasoning, and soy sauce.

Bring soup to a boil, then reduce heat to low and simmer, covered, for 2½–3 hours.

If necessary, add water to the soup. Remove bay leaves before serving.

Yield: 12–15 servings

Kitchen Notes

- This is a good, hearty, nutritious soup, and you don't have to be sick to enjoy it.
- This soup is more flavorful when prepared several days ahead! It freezes well.

Flavorful Tortilla Soup

6 chicken breasts

6 cups water

2 bay leaves

1½ teaspoons salt

1½ teaspoons black pepper

2 onions, chopped

4 cloves garlic, chopped

3 ribs celery, chopped

1 green bell pepper, chopped

1 jalapeño chile pepper, seeded and chopped

2 tablespoons olive oil

1 can tomato soup

1 can Rotel tomatoes

1 teaspoon cumin

2 teaspoons chili powder

1 tablespoon Worcestershire sauce

3 corn tortillas, cut into thin strips

Shredded Cheddar cheese, shredded Monterey Jack cheese, and sour cream, for garnish

In a large stockpot, cook chicken in water with bay leaves, 1 teaspoon salt, 1 teaspoon black pepper, and half of the onions. Bring to a boil, reduce heat, and simmer for 30 minutes.

Turn off heat and allow chicken to cool in broth for 30 minutes. Remove chicken from broth and cut into bite-size pieces. Save broth. This may be done a day ahead of time.

Sauté garlic, celery, bell pepper, jalapeño pepper, and remaining onions in oil for 2 minutes. Add 4 cups broth, tomato soup, tomatoes, cumin, and chili powder.

Simmer on medium heat for 30 minutes.

Add chicken and Worcestershire sauce, remaining ½ teaspoon salt, and remaining ½ teaspoon pepper and cook for 15 minutes. Add tortilla strips and cook for 5 minutes.

Garnish with cheese and a dollop of sour cream.

Yield: 8–10 servings

Kitchen Note

- To make an edible bread bowl like the one in this photo, thaw 1 loaf of frozen bread dough and cut into fourths. Form into balls and let rise, covered, on a nonstick baking pan until doubled in size. Brush tops with beaten egg and bake at 350° for 25 minutes. When cool, cut off the top and hollow out insides before filling with your favorite soup.

Simple Shrimp Chowder

1 tablespoon butter

1 onion, finely chopped

2 10¾-ounce cans cream of potato soup, undiluted

3¼ cups milk

½ teaspoon liquid crab boil

¼ teaspoon cayenne pepper

⅛ teaspoon salt

1½ pounds medium-size fresh or frozen shrimp, thawed

1 cup (4 ounces) shredded Monterey Jack cheese

Melt butter in a heavy soup pan. Sauté onion over medium heat for 5 minutes, or until translucent.

Using a whisk, stir in soup, milk, crab boil, pepper, and salt. Slowly bring to a boil, stirring often.

Add shrimp, reduce heat, and simmer for about 4–5 minutes, or until shrimp turn pink.

Add cheese and stir until melted and blended.

Serve.

Yield: 6–8 servings

Kitchen Note

- For a variation, substitute crawfish for shrimp.

Hearty Chili

1 large onion, chopped

2 tablespoons olive oil

2 cloves garlic

3 pounds coarsely ground lean beef

1 28-ounce can crushed tomatoes

1 can Rotel tomatoes

2 bay leaves, broken

1 teaspoon oregano

2 teaspoons ground cumin

1 teaspoon salt

3 tablespoons chili powder

2 teaspoons black pepper

1 tablespoon Southwest seasoning

2 cups water

2 tablespoons fresh cilantro

1–3 tablespoons all-purpose flour (if needed

for thickening)

Sauté onion and garlic in olive oil until fragrant and opaque.

Cook beef on stove in a heavy soup pot until brown.

Drain browned meat and add to onion and garlic mixture.

Stir in both cans of tomatoes.

Add bay leaves, oregano, cumin, salt, chili powder, black pepper, and Southwest seasoning. Combine well.

Add water, bring to a boil, and reduce heat. Let simmer for 2½–3 hours.

Add cilantro 30 minutes before serving.

If needed, add 1–3 tablespoons flour mixed with ¼ cup water to make a paste to make a thicker chili. If thinner chili is preferred, just add water as needed.

Yield: 10–12 servings

Kitchen Note

- This chili freezes well.

Keep Your Eyes on Pies

P ies are known to disappear from the family table before our very eyes. It doesn't matter if it's savory or sweet, everyone loves a pie! Tastiest Toffee Ice Cream Pie is a favorite of Helen and her son, Martin. They learned to make it when they lived in the sunny California community of Palos Verdes. I created Deep Dish Pizza Pie to please my son William, who wants pizza for every meal. Sweetheart Fudge Pie with a delicious cream cheese crust is a prizewinning recipe from my mom, Mary Lynn Andrews, and Susie Shepherd's Pie is a can't-keep-on-the-shelf item at Aunt Christina's gourmet-to-go shop in New Orleans.

I grew up in a family of four kids and am now blessed to have four of my own. My mom, who was always in the kitchen, taught me to cook for a large family. Cooking for six people was a pleasurable part of her everyday life, and I'm grateful that she passed along her love of cooking for a family to me. When my siblings and I walked in the house after school, there was always some treat waiting for us . . . and it was always homemade. Another thing Mom taught me by example is to make two of everything—especially pie crusts. While the ingredients are out and you're deep into the process, it's just as easy to make "one to serve and one to save." Most all the recipes in this chapter are easy to double.

Since I like to make two of many of my dishes, I've always enjoyed sharing my cooking with friends. I find that the door of a friend's house is always open, especially when you arrive with a homemade treat in hand. One of my favorite dishes to take by a friend's house is chicken pot pie. This recipe has become so popular in our town that I've had friends call me to make one not only for them but for others as well. In a funny turn of events, the recipe got passed around so much that my own family was once the lucky recipient of Comfy Chicken Pot Pie. We didn't even realize it until we sat down for supper and my kids thought it tasted familiar.

Comfy Chicken Pot Pie

⅓ cup margarine or butter

⅓ cup chopped onion

⅓ cup all-purpose flour

½ teaspoon salt

¼ teaspoon black pepper

¼ teaspoon Creole seasoning

1 14-ounce can chicken broth

⅓ cup milk

2½ cups shredded cooked chicken

1¾ cups frozen mixed vegetables, thawed

2 Homemade Pie Crusts (page 167) or ready-made crusts

Heat oven to 425°.

Melt butter in medium saucepan over medium heat. Add onion and cook and stir for 2 minutes, or until tender.

Add flour, salt, pepper, and Creole seasoning and whisk until well blended. Gradually stir in broth and milk, cooking and stirring with a whisk until bubbly and thickened.

Add chicken and vegetables and mix well. Remove from heat.

Line pan with crust, then spoon in chicken-and-vegetable mixture. Top with second crust; seal edges and flute or crimp. Cut slits in several places in top crust.

Bake for 30–40 minutes, or until crust is golden brown. Cover edge of crust with strips of foil during last 15–20 minutes of baking, if necessary, to prevent excessive browning.

Let stand for 5 minutes before serving.

Yield: 6 servings

Kitchen Notes

- After boiling the chicken, save the liquid to use when the recipe calls for chicken broth.

- To seal the edges, press your thumb and index finger against the rim of the pan, then push your other index finger though the space between your thumb and index finger. Another crimping technique is to use the tines of a fork to press around the rim of the pan.

- Individual pot pies are a nice variation.

Susie Shepherd's Pie

FILLING:

2 pounds ground beef

½ cup all-purpose flour

1 tablespoon Creole seasoning

1 tablespoon Italian seasoning

¾ cup chopped onion

½ cup chopped green onions

¼ teaspoon black pepper

3 tablespoons chopped garlic

1½ cups beef broth

TOPPING:

6 cups potatoes, peeled and cubed

2 teaspoons salt plus more to taste

4 tablespoons butter, cut into pieces

1 cup sour cream

¼ cup milk

Salt, to taste

1½–2 cups (6–8 ounces) shredded Cheddar cheese

Fresh parsley, chopped, for garnish

Paprika, for sprinkling on top

TO MAKE FILLING:

Preheat oven to 350°. Coat 2 9-inch glass pie plates with nonstick cooking spray.

Sauté ground beef, adding flour after meat starts to brown.

Add seasonings, onions, pepper, and garlic.

Continue to brown and wilt vegetables, stirring.

Add broth and continue to cook until you have a moist beef mixture that is thick and wet.

Adjust seasoning, then set filling aside.

TO MAKE TOPPING AND ASSEMBLE PIE:

Place potatoes in a large pot with enough water to cover them by a couple of inches. Add 2 teaspoons salt to water. Bring potatoes to a boil, uncovered, over high heat. Cook them for 10–12 minutes.

Coat a baking pan or pie dish with nonstick cooking spray.

Place beef mixture on bottom.

Potatoes are done if easily cut with a butter knife. Drain potatoes in a colander.

Place potatoes in a large mixing bowl and add butter and sour cream. Allow butter to melt and sour cream to warm so ingredients will be easier to blend, then partially mash potatoes with a hand masher or a large fork.

Switch to an electric mixer set at medium speed and continue to mash, adding enough milk to make medium-soft mashed potatoes.

Add salt to taste to potatoes and spoon evenly over beef mixture.

Top with cheese, parsley, and paprika.

Bake for 15–20 minutes, or until thoroughly warmed and cheese is melted.

Yield: 2 pies

Favorite Sloppy Joe Pie

1½ pounds lean ground beef

½ cup sliced green onions

1 15.5-ounce can sloppy joe sauce

1 11-ounce can Mexican whole kernel corn, undrained

1 6-ounce can (5 biscuits) refrigerated buttermilk flaky biscuits

Preheat oven to 375°.

In a large skillet, cook beef and onions until beef is browned and thoroughly cooked, stirring frequently. Drain.

Stir in sauce and corn. Cook for 4–5 minutes, or until thoroughly heated, stirring occasionally. Spoon mixture into an ungreased 9-inch glass pie plate.

Separate biscuits and cut each in half. Arrange cut side down around outside edge of sloppy joe mixture, with sides of biscuits touching.

Bake for 15–20 minutes, or until biscuits are brown.

Yield: 6–8 servings

William's Deep-Dish Pizza Pie

1 pound lean ground beef

¾ cup onion, finely chopped

1 8-ounce jar pizza sauce

1 11-ounce can refrigerated French loaf

1 cup (4 ounces) shredded mozzarella cheese

1 cup (4 ounces) grated Parmesan cheese

1 3-ounce package sliced pepperoni

1 egg

1 tablespoon water

Preheat oven to 350°. Coat a 9-inch glass pie plate with nonstick cooking spray. In a medium skillet, cook ground beef and onion over medium-high heat for 5–7 minutes, or until beef is thoroughly cooked. Drain. Stir in pizza sauce until well mixed.

Carefully unroll dough. Place in pie pan so edges extend over sides of pan. Spoon beef mixture into crust. On top, layer half of the mozzarella and Parmesan, then pepperoni, and then remaining cheese.

In a small bowl, slightly beat egg and water with a fork. Fold extended edges of dough up and over filling and seal edges. Brush crust with egg mixture, using a pastry brush.

Bake for 40 minutes, or until deep golden brown. Cool for 15 minutes. To serve, slice into wedges. Serve with additional pizza sauce, if desired.

Yield: 8 servings

Classic Chicken Spaghetti Pie

2 pounds boneless, skinless chicken breasts

1 bell pepper, finely chopped

2 onions, finely chopped

½ cup finely chopped celery

2 cloves garlic, minced

1 tablespoon butter

1 16-ounce package spaghetti

2 14-ounce cans cream of mushroom soup

1 egg, beaten

⅓ cup slivered almonds

⅓ cup cooking sherry

1 tablespoon Worcestershire sauce

Salt and black pepper, to taste

1 cup (4 ounces) shredded Parmesan cheese

In a large stockpot, cover chicken with water and bring to a boil. Reduce heat and simmer for 20 minutes. Remove chicken, reserving stock. Cool and chop into bite-size pieces.

Preheat oven to 350°.

Lightly grease two 9-inch glass pie plates.

Sauté bell pepper, onions, celery, and garlic in butter until soft, about 2 minutes.

Boil spaghetti in chicken stock until al dente and drain.

Mix spaghetti, soup, egg, sautéed vegetables, and chicken.

Add almonds, sherry, Worcestershire sauce, salt, and black pepper. Mix well. Put in glass pie plates.

Cover with Parmesan.

Bake for 30–40 minutes, or until bubbly.

Yield: 2 pies

Kitchen Notes

- Add sliced mushrooms, if desired, and sauté with other vegetables.
- Great for serving a crowd, this freezes well.
- Make one to serve and one to freeze.

Old-Fashioned Pecan Pie

1 Homemade Pie Crust (page 167)

½ cup light brown sugar

½ cup granulated sugar

3 tablespoons all-purpose flour

1 cup light corn syrup

½ teaspoon vanilla extract

⅛ teaspoon salt

3 eggs

¼ cup butter, melted

1 cup pecan halves

Preheat oven to 300°.

Mix together sugars and flour in a bowl. Use the bottom of your measuring cup like a mortar and pestle to blend ingredients thoroughly. Add corn syrup, vanilla extract, and salt, but do not mix.

Add eggs one at a time, stirring slightly after each.

Fold in butter.

Pour mixture into unbaked crust.

Lay pecan halves on top of filling in circles, beginning at the outside and going in toward the middle.

Bake for 45–55 minutes, or until filling doesn't shake.

Yield: 8 servings

My Oh My Apple Pie

5 cups apples, sliced, peeled, and cored

1½ cups light brown sugar, lightly packed

⅓ cup water

1 cup all-purpose flour

¾ cup butter

1½ teaspoons cinnamon

Preheat oven to 350°.

Place apple slices in a 9-inch glass pie plate that has been coated with nonstick cooking spray.

Sprinkle ½ cup sugar on top of apples.

Pour water over sugar and apples.

Place flour, butter, and cinnamon and remaining 1 cup sugar in food processor. Pulse until crumbly and sprinkle evenly over apples.

Bake for 40–45 minutes.

Yield: 8 servings

Delightful Cheese Pie

FILLING:

2 8-ounce packages cream cheese, softened

2 eggs

1 cup sugar

3 teaspoons vanilla extract

Juice of 1 lemon (1 tablespoon)

1 9-inch Graham Cracker Pie Crust (page 166)

TOPPING:

8 ounces sour cream

1 teaspoon vanilla extract

4 tablespoons sugar

TO MAKE FILLING:

Preheat oven to 350°.

Mix together cream cheese, eggs, sugar, vanilla extract, and lemon juice.

Pour into crust.

Bake for 30–35 minutes, until center does not shake.

Allow to cool in refrigerator for 30 minutes.

TO MAKE TOPPING:

Put sour cream, vanilla extract, and sugar in a bowl and whisk.

Spread mixture over top of cooled pie.

Cook an additional 10 minutes at 350°.

Allow to cool completely before cutting.

Top with your favorite fresh fruit!

Yield: 8 servings

Kitchen Notes

- For ease in blending, bring cream cheese to room temperature.
- For lemon juice, squeeze the lemon over your hand and strain the seeds with your fingers.

Tastiest Toffee Ice Cream Pie

TOFFEE ICE CREAM PIE:

1 Chocolate Wafer Pie Crust (page 166), unbaked

6 ounces chocolate toffee candy bars (Heath bars)

1 pint vanilla ice cream

CHOCOLATE SILK SAUCE:

¼ cup butter, melted

1 cup milk chocolate chips

1¼ cups confectioners' sugar

1 5½-ounce can evaporated milk

1 teaspoon vanilla extract

TO MAKE TOFFEE ICE CREAM PIE:

Prepare crust, but instead of baking it, just refrigerate for 15 minutes to set crust.

Crush candy bars (a few at a time) in a food processor.

Allow ice cream to soften, then mix with chocolate toffee candy bars. Place in crust and freeze.

TO MAKE CHOCOLATE SILK SAUCE:

Melt butter and chocolate chips. Add confectioners' sugar and milk. Stir until smooth.

Cook about 8 minutes, or until thickened. Stir in vanilla extract.

To serve pie, cut into slices and top with warm sauce. This is so rich that a small slice is best.

Extra sauce will keep in a container in refrigerator.

Yield: 8 servings

Kitchen Notes

- Melt butter in a glass dish in the microwave, about 40 to 50 seconds on high for half a stick.
- For crust, stir butter into the crumbs and press in the pan.

Sweetheart Fudge Pie

½ cup butter, softened

¾ cup light brown sugar, lightly packed

3 eggs

1 12-ounce package semisweet chocolate chips, melted

1 teaspoon instant coffee granules

1 teaspoon vanilla extract

½ cup all-purpose flour

1 cup chopped walnuts or pecans

1 9-inch Cream Cheese Pie Crust (opposite page)

Preheat oven to 375°.

Cream butter and gradually add brown sugar. Beat until light and fluffy.

Add eggs one at a time, beating well after each.

Meanwhile, melt chocolate chips in a small, heavy saucepan over medium-low heat.

Slowly pour into egg mixture and continue to mix on medium speed.

Add coffee and vanilla extract. Mix well.

Turn mixer on low and stir in flour and nuts.

Pour into unbaked crust.

Bake for 30 minutes.

Yield: 8 servings

Cream Cheese Pie Crust

1 cup all-purpose flour

¼ cup confectioners' sugar

Pinch of salt

½ cup unsalted butter, cold, cubed

4 ounces cream cheese, cold, cubed

Blend dry ingredients in food processor fitted with a steel blade or a standing mixer with a paddle.

Add butter and cream cheese and mix just until dough forms around blade or paddle. Wrap dough in plastic, flatten into a disk, and chill 30 minutes.

Roll dough on lightly floured surface to 14 inches in diameter and ¼ inch thick.

Flip and turn it often to prevent sticking.

Fold into quarters, then unfold into a lightly greased 9-inch pie plate. Adjust dough to fit, pressing lightly against bottom and sides of pan. Try not to stretch it, or it will shrink. Trim all but 1 inch of overhang with scissors. Fold edge under and crimp.

Freeze until firm, 15 minutes.

Preheat oven to 400°. Line frozen shell with foil, pressing firmly against sides and folding gently over edges. Fill shell with raw rice or dried beans to keep bottom from puffing up, and bake until crust is set but not browned, about 20 minutes.

Unfold foil at edges and carefully lift it out, then return shell to oven. Bake for 5–10 minutes, or until pale golden.

Fill as directed in recipes.

Yield: 1 crust, with enough extra for lattice or decorative topping

Kitchen Note

● To crimp the edges of the crust, press prongs of a fork around the edge.

Graham Cracker Pie Crust

2 cups finely ground graham crackers (about 30 squares)

½ cup unsalted butter, melted

In a mixing bowl, combine graham crackers and butter with a fork until evenly moistened.

Lightly grease the bottom and sides of 9-inch pie pan.

Pour crumbs into pan and, using the bottom of a measuring cup or glass, press crumbs down into base and 1 inch up sides.

Refrigerate for 15 minutes.

Yield: 1 crust

Kitchen Notes

- This crust recipe is easy to double.
- Put crackers and wafers in a plastic storage bag and crush using your hands or a rolling pin.

Chocolate Wafer Pie Crust

1 18-ounce package Oreos or chocolate wafer cookies

6 tablespoons butter

Preheat oven to 350°.

Lightly grease a 9-inch pie pan.

Crush cookies until they are fine crumbs. This can be done in the food processor.

Melt butter.

Mix butter with cookies.

Pour crumbs into the pan and, using the bottom of a measuring cup or glass, press crumbs down into base and 1 inch up sides.

Bake for 10 minutes.

Yield: 1 crust

Homemade Pie Crust

1 teaspoon salt

2 cups all-purpose flour

⅔ cup chilled shortening (for buttery-flavored crust, use butter-flavored shortening)

¼ cup cold water

Add salt to flour.

In a large bowl, mix flour and shortening with a pastry blender or work lightly with tips of fingers. Do this until crumbly.

Add cold water slowly to bowl of dough and mix well.

Gather dough into large ball. Handle lightly to incorporate as much air as possible. This will make a flaky crust.

Lightly flour a work surface and roll dough to a 14-inch round about ⅛ inch thick. (If using a pastry cloth, less flour is needed on work surface.)

Dust rolling pin and dough with flour as needed. (If dough has been refrigerated, bring to room temperature.) Roll from center out. Roll continuously in the same direction, lifting rolling pin and moving back to center to roll again.

Fold into quarters, then unfold into a lightly greased 9-inch pie plate. Press lightly against bottom and sides of dish. Trim all but 1 inch of overhang with scissors, fold edge under, and crimp.

If your crust tears, patch together gently with your fingers, using excess dough from another part of the crust—do not reroll.

Yield: 1 crust

Kitchen Notes

- Work shortening into flour using a wire pastry blender, two table knives, or your fingers. This tenderizes the pastry.

- Dough should form a ball that is firm and not too wet.

- Remember to press down on the dough with the rolling pin and start in the center of the ball, rolling out to the north, south, east, and west.

- Too much shortening makes the crust greasy.

- Too much flour makes it tough.

- Too much water makes it soggy.

Bake Sale Favorites

Granny's Cheese Straws

Leslie's Fluffy Ladies

Conglomerations

La-Te-Dahs!

Rob's Ranger
Cookies

Helen's Peanut Butter
M&M Cookies

Gingersnaps

Glazed Sugar Cookies

Mrs. Todd's Cream-Cheese
Pound Cake

Grandmother's No-Fail
Pumpkin Bread

Tunnel of Fudge Cake

Royal Carrot Cake

Poppy Seed Bread

So Good Banana Bread

Sterling's Simply Spectacular
Brownies

Kim's Raspberry Bars

When we were little girls, a popular television commercial of the day claimed "Nothing says lovin' like something from the oven." This simple saying cleverly expressed a universal truth: Nothing warms the heart and fills the home like the aroma of baking. The recipes in this chapter are family recipes that were cooked with love in our grandmothers' and mothers' kitchens. We couldn't write a cookbook without including them. My grandmother Helen Todd of Hattiesburg, Mississippi, and my mother, Dorothy Puckett, as well as Leslie's grandmother Annette Shepherd of New Orleans and her mother, Mary Lynn Andrews, believed that children should not only be seen and heard but welcome in the family kitchen. Just as they were handed down to us, these recipes are passed along to you in hopes that they will create magical food memories for your family as they did for ours.

All of my friends know that if I'm coming to visit or asked to bring something, more than likely it will be my grandmother's pound cake. In my travels as a cooking teacher, I have carried many a pound cake around the country. The secret to delivering the perfect pound cake is to wrap it in plastic after baking, place it in a plastic storage bag, and put it in the freezer. I put a note to myself on the back door that says "Don't forget the pound cake." As I am leaving for the airport, I place the pound cake in my suitcase, and when I arrive at my destination, it is perfect. On a recent trip, I delivered Mississippi-made pound cakes to California and Illinois. First stop was the Napa Valley, where I left one on the kitchen table of family friend, author, and hostess extraordinaire Molly Chappellet. My idea was that a piece of pound cake and a glass of milk would be a welcome respite from the weekend of visitors and myriad activities. My next stop was Chicago, where I hoped to see my friend Art Smith, whose busy schedule with his restaurant and duties as Oprah's personal chef made finding a time to meet almost impossible. When Art learned I had brought a pound cake for him, he suddenly found a way to make our schedules work. My grandmother's pound cake is special because it was her cherished recipe, and when she made it for me, she made it with love. That's the most important ingredient of all . . . and one I never forget to add.

Granny's Cheese Straws

1 cup margarine, at room temperature

12 ounces (3 cups) shredded extrasharp Cheddar cheese

2 cups all-purpose flour

⅛ teaspoon salt

½ teaspoon cayenne pepper

Preheat oven to 350°.

Cream margarine and cheese in mixer on medium-high speed for 5 minutes, or until very creamy.

Sift flour, salt, and pepper and gradually add to creamed mixture.

Place dough in a cookie press and make long strips on a cookie sheet.

Bake for 8–10 minutes.

Remove from oven.

With a table knife, cut into 3–4-inch "straws."

When cool, remove from pan with a spatula. Store in an airtight container.

Yield: 4–5 dozen

Kitchen Notes

- Butter and cheese should be very creamy before adding the flour.
- Leslie's mom, who gave us this recipe, says using margarine instead of butter is the key to success.

Leslie's Fluffy Ladies

1 roll refrigerated chocolate chip cookie dough

6 ounces semisweet chocolate chips

1 12-ounce bag caramels

3 tablespoons half and half

1 cup chopped pecans

Preheat oven to 350°.

Grease a 9- by 13-inch baking dish.

Press cookie dough into baking dish and bake according to dough directions.

Sprinkle with chocolate chips and bake for about 5 minutes more.

Meanwhile, unwrap caramels and put in a pan, then add half and half.

Stir caramels and half and half over medium heat until caramels are melted.

Pour over chocolate chips and spread evenly.

Sprinkle with chopped pecans.

Put in refrigerator to cool.

Cut into bars when completely cool.

Yield: 24 2-inch squares

Kitchen Notes

- Waxed paper works great for pressing the dough into the pan.
- When the bars are cool, you can individually wrap them for a bake sale.

Conglomerations

12 graham crackers

1 cup butter

1½ cups crunchy or creamy peanut butter

A little less than 1 pound confectioners' sugar, sifted

6 1.55-ounce Hershey milk chocolate bars

Preheat oven to 400°.

Line a 9- by 13-inch pan with aluminum foil.

Place graham crackers side by side on the foil.

Melt butter in a saucepan. Add peanut butter and confectioners' sugar to saucepan.

Mix until peanut butter and confectioners' sugar are completely combined. Remove from stove top.

Spread peanut butter mixture over graham crackers.

Break chocolate bars into pieces and lay them over peanut butter mixture.

Bake for 5–7 minutes, or until chocolate softens.

Remove from oven and spread chocolate all over.

Place in refrigerator to cool before cutting.

Conglomerations will keep at room temperature until they are all gone—which won't take very long!

Yield: 24 2-inch squares

NOTE: Chocolate and cinnamon graham crackers work just as well as the original graham crackers.

La-Te-Dahs!

2 cups unsalted butter

1 cup dark brown sugar, packed

1 cup light brown sugar, packed

3 large eggs, beaten

1 tablespoon vanilla extract

2 tablespoons cinnamon

½ teaspoon ground ginger

2 cups granulated sugar

2 cups all-purpose flour

2 teaspoons salt

2 teaspoons baking soda

3 cups quick-cooking oats

2 cups walnut pieces

1 cup raisins

Preheat oven to 350°.

Line cookie sheets with parchment paper.

Cream together butter and brown sugars until light and fluffy.

Add eggs and vanilla extract.

Combine cinnamon, ginger, and granulated sugar and add slowly to creamed mixture.

Sift together flour, salt, and baking soda and slowly add to sugar mixture.

Blend in oats, then stir in walnuts and raisins.

Drop by rounded tablespoons onto cookie sheets, about 2 inches apart.

Bake for 9–11 minutes.

Remove cookie sheets from oven and bang sharply on the counter. Remove cookies with a spatula, and place them on a brown paper bag to cool. (This step is very important!)

Yield: 24 2-inch squares

Kitchen Note

- When you measure brown sugar, you must "pack" according to the directions. When the recipe calls for "packed," you press the brown sugar into the measuring cup to the desired unit of measure. "Lightly packed" means to scoop the sugar into the measuring cup to the desired measuring line with no pressing or packing. Of course, there is less sugar in a lightly packed measure.

Rob's Ranger Cookies

1 cup butter-flavored shortening

1 cup granulated sugar

1 cup light brown sugar, lightly packed

2 eggs

1 teaspoon vanilla extract

2 cups all-purpose flour

1 teaspoon baking soda

1 teaspoon baking powder

½ teaspoon salt

2 cups quick-cooking oats

2 cups crispy rice cereal

Preheat oven to 350°.

Grease a cookie sheet or line with parchment paper.

Cream shortening and sugars together.

Add eggs and vanilla extract and mix until smooth.

Sift flour, baking soda, baking powder, and salt together and add to creamed mixture. Mix well.

Add oats and cereal and mix.

For each cookie, drop heaping tablespoons of dough onto cookie sheet, about ½ inch apart, and press slightly.

Bake for 8–10 minutes.

Yield: 6 dozen

Kitchen Note

- Cream the shortening and sugar for about 4 to 5 minutes, until they're really creamy.

Helen's Peanut Butter M&M Cookies

2 cups all-purpose flour

1 teaspoon baking soda

1 teaspoon salt

¼ teaspoon cinnamon

¾ cup unsalted butter, softened

¾ cup peanut butter

1 cup sugar

1 cup light brown sugar, lightly packed

2 eggs

1 teaspoon vanilla extract

¼ cup milk

2 cups old-fashioned oats (not quick cooking)

12 -ounce bag M&Ms baking bits

Preheat oven to 325°.

Lightly grease a baking sheet or line with parchment paper.

Sift flour, baking soda, salt, and cinnamon. Set aside.

In a large bowl, cream butter, peanut butter, and sugars.

Beat in eggs one at a time. Add vanilla extract.

Add milk and flour mixture. Beat until well blended.

Stir in the oats and baking bits.

Drop by rounded tablespoons onto baking sheet, about 2 inches apart.

Bake for 10–12 minutes.

Let sit for a minute before moving to a cooling rack.

Yield: 2 dozen

Kitchen Note

- Make giant cookies by putting 2 tablespoons of dough together on the baking sheet.

Gingersnaps

¾ cup butter, softened

1 cup sugar plus more for rolling

¼ cup molasses

¼ teaspoon salt

1 teaspoon cinnamon

2 teaspoons baking soda

1 teaspoon cloves

1 teaspoon ginger

2 cups all-purpose flour

Preheat oven to 350°.

Lightly grease a baking sheet or line with parchment.

Cream together butter and sugar. Add molasses and mix thoroughly.

Add salt, cinnamon, baking soda, cloves, and ginger and mix well.

Sift flour and add to the mix. Form dough into 1-inch balls and roll in sugar. Place on baking sheet, about 2 inches apart.

Bake for 10–12 minutes.

Yield: about 2 dozen

Kitchen Notes

- To soften butter, let it come to room temperature at least an hour before you begin to make the cookies.

- Roll the dough into balls. Place about ½ cup of sugar in a shallow bowl and roll the dough balls in the sugar. Add more sugar as needed.

Gingersnaps (opposite), Helen's Peanut Butter M&M Cookies (page 175), and Glazed Sugar Cookies (page 178)

Glazed Sugar Cookies

COOKIES:

1 cup butter, softened

1½ cups sugar

2 teaspoons cream of tartar

1 teaspoon baking soda

¼ teaspoon salt

2 eggs

1 teaspoon vanilla extract

2½ cups all-purpose flour

GLAZE:

3–4 teaspoons milk

1 teaspoon vanilla extract

½ teaspoon almond extract

1 cup confectioners' sugar

Assorted food coloring

Sprinkles (optional)

TO MAKE COOKIES:

Preheat oven to 375°. In a large bowl, cream butter for 30 seconds. Blend in sugar, cream of tartar, baking soda, and salt. Beat in eggs and vanilla extract. Mix in as much of the flour as possible with mixer. Use a wooden spoon to stir in any remaining flour.

Cover and chill 1 hour, or until dough is firm. Shape dough into 1-inch balls and place 2 inches apart on ungreased cookie sheet.

Bake 8–10 minutes, or until edges are lightly brown. Let cool and decorate with colored glaze as desired.

TO MAKE GLAZE:

Combine milk and extracts, then stir in confectioners' sugar. Add a bit more milk to thin or more confectioners' sugar to stiffen. Blend in 3–4 drops food coloring or, if desired, divide glaze among separate small bowls and tint each a different color with 1–2 drops of food coloring.

Use a spoon to pour and spread over cookies. Add sprinkles, if desired.

Yield: about 3 dozen

Kitchen Notes

- Refrigerate the dough so it will be easier to roll into balls.
- For the glaze, stir all ingredients together using a whisk. Pick out your favorite food coloring and tint the icing, or you can use several colors by dividing the icing into different bowls and tinting separately.
- When making holiday cookies, this glaze works well as an icing.

Mrs. Todd's Cream-Cheese Pound Cake

3 cups sugar

1½ cups butter, softened

8 ounces cream cheese, softened

3 cups all-purpose flour

½ teaspoon salt

6 eggs

1 tablespoon lemon extract

1 tablespoon almond extract

Preheat oven to 325°.

Grease and flour a 10-inch tube pan or Bundt pan.

In a large bowl, cream sugar, butter, and cream cheese until light and fluffy.

Sift flour and salt together.

Alternately add eggs and flour to creamed mixture, beginning and ending with flour.

Add flavorings.

Beat until smooth and blended.

Bake for 1 hour 15 minutes.

Cool before removing from pan.

Yield: 10–12 servings

Kitchen Note

● This cake freezes well. Wrap it in plastic, place in a storage bag, and freeze.

Grandmother's No-Fail Pumpkin Bread

3 cups all-purpose flour

½ teaspoon baking soda

1 teaspoon salt

1 teaspoon cinnamon

1 teaspoon nutmeg

3 cups sugar

1 cup canola oil or vegetable oil

3 eggs

2 cups canned pumpkin

Preheat oven to 325°.

Grease two 9- by 5- by 3-inch loaf pans.

Sift together flour, baking soda, salt, cinnamon, and nutmeg and set aside.

In a large mixing bowl, blend sugar and oil. Add eggs one at a time and beat well, using a whisk.

Mix pumpkin into egg mixture.

Add sifted dry ingredients and mix thoroughly.

Pour batter into loaf pans and let stand for 20 minutes.

Bake for an hour and a half, or until done.

Yield: 2 large loaves

Kitchen Notes

- This one-bowl wonder is easy to double.
- Wrap in plastic, tie on a bow, and give as a gift.

Tunnel of Fudge Cake

CAKE:

1¾ cups butter, softened

1¾ cups sugar

6 eggs

2 cups confectioners' sugar

2¼ cups all-purpose flour

¾ cup cocoa powder

2 cups chopped walnuts

GLAZE:

¾ cup powdered sugar

¼ cup cocoa powder

3½–4 tablespoons milk

TO MAKE CAKE:

Preheat oven to 350°.

Grease and flour a Bundt pan.

In a large bowl, beat butter and sugar until light and fluffy. Add eggs one at a time, beating well after each one.

Gradually add confectioners' sugar and blend well. Sift flour. By hand, stir in sifted flour, cocoa, and walnuts. Spoon batter into pan, spreading evenly.

Bake for 40–45 minutes. Cool upright in pan on cooling rack 1 hour, then invert onto serving plate. Cool completely.

TO MAKE GLAZE:

In a small bowl, combine glaze ingredients until well blended. Spoon over top of cake, allowing some to run down sides.

Store tightly covered.

Yield: 16 servings

Kitchen Notes

- Since this cake has a soft tunnel of fudge, ordinary doneness test cannot be used. Accurate oven temperature and bake time are critical.
- Combine the glaze ingredients while the cake is cooling.
- Nuts are essential for the success of the recipe.

Royal Carrot Cake

PECAN CREAM FILLING:

1½ cups sugar

¼ cup all-purpose flour

¾ teaspoon salt

1½ cups heavy cream

¾ cup butter

1¼ cups chopped pecans

2 teaspoons vanilla extract

CARROT CAKE:

1¼ cups corn oil

2 cups sugar

2 cups all-purpose flour

2 teaspoons cinnamon

2 teaspoons baking powder

1 teaspoon baking soda

1 teaspoon salt

4 eggs, room temperature

4 cups grated carrots (about a 1-pound bag)

1 cup pecans, chopped

1 cup raisins

CREAM CHEESE FROSTING:

8 ounces butter, softened

8 ounces cream cheese, softened

1 1-pound box confectioners' sugar

1 tablespoon vanilla extract

ASSEMBLY:

1½ cups sweetened shredded coconut

TO MAKE PECAN CREAM FILLING:

Combine sugar, flour, and salt in a heavy saucepan. Slowly whisk in cream. Add butter.

Over low heat, cook and stir mixture until butter melts. Continue to cook for 20 minutes, stirring occasionally. Filling should be brown in color.

Cool for 15 minutes.

Stir in pecans and vanilla extract.

Allow to cool completely and then refrigerate, preferably overnight.

If mixture is too thick to spread when ready to use, bring it to room temperature.

TO MAKE CARROT CAKE:

Preheat oven to 350°.

Grease and flour a 10-inch tube cake pan.

In a large bowl, whisk oil and sugar together.

In a separate bowl, sift flour, cinnamon, baking powder, baking soda, and salt together.

Blend half of the sifted ingredients into the sugar-oil mixture.

Add eggs one by one, alternating with remaining dry ingredients. Combine well using a whisk.

Add carrots, pecans, and raisins.

Pour into tube pan and bake for 1 hour 10 minutes.

Cool upright in the pan on a cooling rack.

TO MAKE CREAM CHEESE FROSTING:

Cream butter until light and fluffy.

Add cream cheese and beat until well blended.

Sift confectioners' sugar and add to butter mixture. Mix until well blended.

Add vanilla extract and mix well.

Refrigerate if not using immediately, but bring to a spreadable temperature before using.

TO ASSEMBLE:

Preheat oven to 300°.

Spread coconut on a baking sheet and bake for 10–15 minutes, stirring occasionally, until it lightly colors. Cool.

Have filling and frosting at a spreadable consistency.

Loosen cake in its pan and invert onto a serving plate.

Carefully split cake into 3 horizontal layers using a long serrated knife.

Spread filling between layers.

Spread frosting over top and sides.

Pat toasted coconut onto sides of cake.

Yield: 12 servings

Poppy Seed Bread

2 cups sugar

1¼ cups vegetable oil

4 eggs

4 cups all-purpose flour

4 teaspoons baking powder

1 teaspoon salt

1 12-ounce can evaporated milk

1 teaspoon vanilla extract

½ cup poppy seeds

Preheat oven to 325°.

Grease 2 large loaf pans.

Beat sugar and oil on medium speed until thoroughly blended.

Add eggs one at a time, beating after each.

Sift flour, baking powder, and salt and slowly add them to sugar mixture.

Add evaporated milk and mix until blended.

Stir in vanilla extract and poppy seeds.

Pour batter into loaf pans.

Bake for 35 minutes, or until lightly browned.

Yield: 2 large loaves

So Good Banana Bread

½ cup shortening

½ cup butter, at room temperature

2 cups sugar

1 cup light brown sugar, lightly packed

2 teaspoons vanilla extract

4 eggs

½ teaspoon salt

3½ cups all-purpose flour

2 teaspoons baking soda

½ cup buttermilk

6 small bananas, mashed

1 cup pecans, chopped (optional)

Preheat oven to 350°.

Grease 2 loaf pans.

In a large bowl, cream shortening, butter, sugars, and vanilla extract until fluffy.

Add eggs one at a time, blending thoroughly after each addition.

In a separate bowl, sift salt, flour, and baking soda twice.

Add dry ingredients alternately with buttermilk to creamy mixture.

Combine bananas and pecans and blend into mixture.

Pour into loaf pans and bake for 55–60 minutes.

Yield: 2 loaves

Kitchen Note

- Overly ripe bananas work best.

Sterling's Simply Spectacular Brownies

1 cup butter

2½ cups sugar

2 squares unsweetened baking chocolate

1 square semisweet baking chocolate

1½ cups all-purpose flour

½ teaspoon baking powder

4 eggs

2 teaspoons vanilla extract

2 pinches of salt

Preheat oven to 300°.

Lightly grease two 8-inch-square brownie pans. (If you use one large pan, the batter will thin out too much.)

Melt butter, sugar, and chocolates in medium (2-quart) saucepan on top of stove. Stir well with a spatula with a square front, as this is flexible and will not let anything accrue on the bottom of the pan. (You can use a wooden spoon if you do not have a heat-tolerant spatula.) Remove from heat.

Double-sift flour, add baking powder, and set aside.

Break eggs into saucepan of chocolate when it has cooled a little. (You may want to break into a bowl first, just in case you get any shells.)

Stir well, using a hand mixer if necessary.

Add vanilla extract and salt to chocolate in saucepan. Stir well.

Add double-sifted flour to chocolate in saucepan. Stir well.

Split chocolate mixture evenly between the two pans.

Bake for 40 minutes. Remove immediately, even if they do not seem done.

Let sit in pan for 5–8 minutes but no longer or they will overcook.

Cut into 16 brownies per pan. Be careful because they will still be hot.

Yield: 32 brownies

Kitchen Note

● A spatula is the best tool to take the brownies out of the pan.

Kim's Raspberry Bars

CRUST:

1¼ cups all-purpose flour

⅓ cup light brown sugar, lightly packed

½ cup (1 stick) butter, cold and cut into 8 pieces

1¼ cup raspberry preserves, seedless, or apricot preserves

TOPPING:

¾ cup all-purpose flour

1½ cups light brown sugar, lightly packed

¼ cup (½ stick) butter, cold and cut into 4 pieces

⅛ teaspoon salt

1 teaspoon almond extract

ICING:

1 cup powdered sugar

1 tablespoon milk

TO MAKE CRUST:

Preheat oven to 350°. Grease a jelly-roll pan.

Put flour, brown sugar, and butter into a food processor. Pulse until butter is completely mixed into the flour and sugar. Pat evenly into pan.

Bake for 10 minutes. Remove from oven and cool.

TO MAKE TOPPING:

Place topping ingredients in food processor and pulse until completely combined.

TO ASSEMBLE BARS:

Spread preserves thinly all across the cooled crust.

Sprinkle topping all over preserves.

Bake for 12 to 15 minutes. Cool.

TO MAKE ICING:

Combine icing ingredients and stir until blended. Drizzle over cooled bars.

Cut into squares and enjoy!

Yield: 24 2-inch squares

Safety Tips

Many recipes in this book are easy enough for kids to make. However, it's best to keep the following general "rules" in mind.

- Wash hands before and after handling raw meat and chicken.
- Always have an adult helper when cooking on the stove top.
- Ask for help when placing a pan into the oven or removing it.
- Ask for help when using a sharp knife.
- When draining potatoes, pasta, or vegetables, always ask an adult helper to take the hot pan to the sink or pour hot water through the colander.
- When using an electric hand mixer, be sure to keep the beaters in the mixture until you turn the mixer off. Otherwise you will be wiping off the kitchen cabinets and walls.

TECHNIQUES TO REMEMBER

- Separating eggs is not a hard thing to do. Have two bowls ready. With one hand, tap the egg on the edge of the bowl, making an even crack. Then, using both hands, pull the edges apart until the whole egg is now in two parts. Some of the white will instantly fall into the bowl underneath it. That bowl is for egg whites only. Pour the rest of the egg back and forth from one shell half to the other, allowing the egg white to fall into the whites-only bowl. When only yolk remains in the shell, pour it into the other bowl—the yolks-only bowl. Should you get yolk into the white, try to remove it with the corner of a paper towel.
- To beat eggs, crack eggs in a bowl and beat with a whisk or fork.
- Creaming means to beat butter and sugar together until they are fluffy. You can do this with a hand mixer or a standing mixer.
- When folding in the sifted flour mixture, use a rubber spatula. Scoop batter from the bottom of the bowl, then up the side of the bowl and up to the top. Repeat, turning the bowl, until the batter looks blended.
- To grease a pan, rub about 1 tablespoon of butter all over the inside of the pan with your fingertips. You can also use a paper towel.

- A double boiler is used to cook foods that scorch and burn easily on direct heat. You can make your own double boiler if you do not own one. Put about 1 inch of water in a saucepan and rest a heat-resistant bowl that fits snugly in the saucepan, leaving 2 to 3 inches between the bottom of the bowl and the saucepan. Place the food to be melted in the bowl. Remember to use a liquid measuring cup when measuring liquid ingredients such as water, olive oil, and peanut oil.

- When grating foods like onions or chocolate, always use a downward motion on the grater. Be careful at the end not to scrape your fingers on the grater—ouch!

- Use a garlic press to crush garlic.

- Carrots are hard to cut. You do the peeling, and let an adult do the cutting. Remember to always peel a carrot with a downward motion, turning the carrot as needed.

- Cooked chicken can be cut with a plastic knife or table knife.

- When skewering chicken, be careful not to stick yourself with the sharp end of the skewer.

Authors' Bios

Helen Puckett DeFrance was born and raised in Jackson, Mississippi. The fourth child in a family of six children, she learned cooking from her grandmother, Helen Todd. Helen combined a passion for cooking with an unparalleled gift for teaching to create the Camp Blackberry cooking program for kids at the prestigious Blackberry Farm near Knoxville, Tennessee (where she's been a featured guest chef for holiday events since 2002). A graduate of the master's program at Pepperdine University with a specialty in Montessori training (a hands-on, experiential teaching method), she presents her cooking program, THYME to Cook!, in schools across the country, as well as at the Everyday Gourmet in her hometown, Viking Cooking Schools nationwide, and Blackberry Farm, among others. She lives in Jackson with her son, Martin, along with her two dogs, Eddie and Henri.

Leslie Andrews Carpenter was born in Greenville, Mississippi, the eldest of four, to two New Orleans natives, to whom she attributes her love of food, family, and cooking. A former Miss Ole Miss, Leslie also worked in catering for the world-famous Windsor Court in New Orleans and ran a successful catering business out of her home for 6 years before she began teaching cooking classes at the Everyday Gourmet. She also teaches at Viking Cooking Schools around the country, among others. She lives in Jackson with her husband, Phillip, and their four children, Rob, William, Myers, and Annie.

Carol Puckett, the writer of this book, is president of the Viking Hospitality Group, a division of Viking Range Corporation. She is also the founder of the Everyday Gourmet, a Jackson-based cooking store and cooking school, and owner of a companion store, the Everyday Gardener. She serves on the board of directors of the International Ballet Competition, the Southern Food and Beverage Museum, the Southern Foodways Alliance, and the Center for the Study of Southern Culture. When not cooking, eating, writing, or talking about food, she enjoys hiking, fishing, canoeing, and living the life of a Sweet Potato Queen.

Index

Underscored page references indicate kitchen notes. **Boldfaced** page references indicate photographs.

Conversion Chart

These equivalents have been slightly rounded to make measuring easier.

Volume Measurements

U.S.	Imperial	Metric
¼ tsp	–	1 ml
½ tsp	–	2 ml
1 tsp	–	5 ml
1 Tbsp	–	15 ml
2 Tbsp (1 oz)	1 fl oz	30 ml
¼ cup (2 oz)	2 fl oz	60 ml
⅓ cup (3 oz)	3 fl oz	80 ml
½ cup (4 oz)	4 fl oz	120 ml
⅔ cup (5 oz)	5 fl oz	160 ml
¾ cup (6 oz)	6 fl oz	180 ml
1 cup (8 oz)	8 fl oz	240 ml

Weight Measurements

U.S.	Metric
1 oz	30 g
2 oz	60 g
4 oz (¼ lb)	115 g
5 oz (⅓ lb)	145 g
6 oz	170 g
7 oz	200 g
8 oz (½ lb)	230 g
10 oz	285 g
12 oz (¾ lb)	340 g
14 oz	400 g
16 oz (1 lb)	455 g
2.2 lb	1 kg

Length Measurements

U.S.	Metric
¼"	0.6 cm
½"	1.25 cm
1"	2.5 cm
2"	5 cm
4"	11 cm
6"	15 cm
8"	20 cm
10"	25 cm
12" (1')	30 cm

Pan Sizes

U.S.	Metric
8" cake pan	20 × 4 cm sandwich or cake tin
9" cake pan	23 × 3.5 cm sandwich or cake tin
11" × 7" baking pan	28 × 18 cm baking tin
13" × 9" baking pan	32.5 × 23 cm baking tin
15" × 10" baking pan	38 × 25.5 cm baking tin (Swiss roll tin)
1½ qt baking dish	1.5 liter baking dish
2 qt baking dish	2 liter baking dish
2 qt rectangular baking dish	30 × 19 cm baking dish
9" pie plate	22 × 4 or 23 × 4 cm pie plate
7" or 8" springform pan	18 or 20 cm springform or loose-bottom cake tin
9" × 5" loaf pan	23 × 13 cm or 2 lb narrow loaf tin or pâté tin

Temperatures

Fahrenheit	Centigrade	Gas
140°	60°	–
160°	70°	–
180°	80°	–
225°	105°	¼
250°	120°	½
275°	135°	1
300°	150°	2
325°	160°	3
350°	180°	4
375°	190°	5
400°	200°	6
425°	220°	7
450°	230°	8
475°	245°	9
500°	260°	–

Saturday Morning Breakfast

Fluffy Pancakes

- [ ] 4 tbsp. butter
- [ ] 2 cups milk
- [ ] 2 eggs
- [ ] 2 cups flour
- [ ] ½ tsp. salt
- [ ] 3 tbsp. sugar
- [ ] 2 tsp. baking powder

Sausage Pinwheels

- [ ] 1 16-oz. roll sausage (mild or hot)
- [ ] 1 recipe Homemade Buttermilk Biscuits

Homemade Buttermilk Biscuits

- [ ] 4 cups all-purpose flour
- [ ] 1½ tsp. baking powder
- [ ] ½ tsp. baking soda
- [ ] 1 tsp. salt
- [ ] 1 cup shortening or butter
- [ ] 2 cups buttermilk

Get Up & Go! Breakfast

Wacky Waffles

- [ ] 3 eggs
- [ ] 1 cup club soda
- [ ] ½ cup buttermilk
- [ ] 1 tsp. baking soda
- [ ] 1¾ cups all-purpose flour
- [ ] 2 tsp. baking powder
- [ ] ½ tsp. salt
- [ ] ½ cup vegetable oil
- [ ] Nonstick cooking spray

On-the-Go A.M. Breakfast Sandwich

- [ ] 1 recipe "Bomber" Biscuits, or 1 10.2-oz. can refrigerated buttermilk biscuits
- [ ] 6 eggs
- [ ] 1 tsp. salt
- [ ] ½ tsp. pepper
- [ ] 3 tbsp. milk

- [ ] ¾ cup (about 4 oz.) cooked ham or bacon
- [ ] 1 tbsp. butter
- [ ] ½ cup cheddar cheese, shredded

"Bomber" Biscuits

- [ ] 4½ cups biscuit mix
- [ ] 8 oz. sour cream
- [ ] 1 cup club soda
- [ ] ¼ cup butter

Made-with-Love Blueberry Muffins

- [ ] ⅔ cup shortening
- [ ] 1 cup sugar
- [ ] 3 eggs
- [ ] 3 cups flour
- [ ] 2½ tsp. baking powder
- [ ] 1 tsp. salt
- [ ] 1 cup milk
- [ ] 2 cups blueberries

Lazy Morning Brunch

Overnight Oven-Baked French Toast

- [ ] ¼ cup butter
- [ ] 12 ¾-inch-thick slices of French bread
- [ ] 6 eggs
- [ ] 1½ cups milk
- [ ] ¼ cup sugar
- [ ] 2 tbsp. maple syrup
- [ ] 1 tsp. vanilla extract
- [ ] ½ tsp. salt
- [ ] Powdered sugar

Crispy Brown-Sugar Bacon

- [ ] 1 lb. regular sliced bacon
- [ ] 1 cup light brown sugar
- [ ] 1 tbsp. cracked black pepper (optional)

Cheddar Cheese Grits

- [ ] 1 quart milk
- [ ] ¼ cup butter

- [ ] 1 cup uncooked grits
- [ ] 1 tsp. salt
- [ ] ½ tsp. ground pepper
- [ ] 1 egg
- [ ] 8 oz. sharp cheddar cheese, grated
- [ ] ½ cup Parmesan cheese, grated

Absolutely Delicious Danish

- [ ] 2 8-oz. cans crescent dinner rolls
- [ ] 16 oz. cream cheese
- [ ] 1½ cups sugar
- [ ] 1 egg
- [ ] 1 tsp. vanilla extract
- [ ] 1 tsp. almond extract
- [ ] ½ cup butter
- [ ] 1 tsp. ground cinnamon
- [ ] 1 cup almonds, chopped (optional)

Make-and-Take Picnic Lunch

Greek Wraps

- [ ] ½ cup plain yogurt
- [ ] 2 tbsp. lemon juice
- [ ] 1 tbsp. white wine vinegar
- [ ] ½ tsp. dried oregano
- [ ] ½ tsp. salt
- [ ] ½ garlic clove
- [ ] ½ tsp. pepper
- [ ] ½ tsp. Greek seasoning
- [ ] 6 chicken breasts
- [ ] 2 cups romaine lettuce
- [ ] 1 cup tomatoes
- [ ] ½ cup cucumber
- [ ] ½ cup feta cheese
- [ ] ¼ cup ripe olives, sliced
- [ ] ¼ cup purple onion
- [ ] 10–12 soft flour tortillas

Gouda Pimento Cheese Wraps

- [ ] 2 pounds of Gouda (or smoked Gouda) cheese
- [ ] 2 3-oz. jars of pimento
- [ ] 1¼ cups mayonnaise

- [ ] 1 small white onion
- [ ] 1 tsp. black pepper
- [ ] Pinch of salt
- [ ] 10-12 soft tortillas

Chinese Chicken Wraps

- [ ] 1 6-oz. pkg. slivered almonds
- [ ] ¼ cup sesame seeds
- [ ] 1 pkg. ramen noodles
- [ ] 2 tbsp. butter
- [ ] 6 chicken breasts, cooked
- [ ] ½ head iceberg lettuce
- [ ] 4 green onions
- [ ] ¼ cup cilantro
- [ ] 2 tbsp. sesame oil
- [ ] ¼ cup rice vinegar
- [ ] ¼ cup soy sauce
- [ ] 1 tsp. salt
- [ ] ½ tsp. pepper
- [ ] 1 tsp. sugar
- [ ] 1 tbsp. garlic chili sauce
- [ ] 10–12 soft flour tortillas

Fruitini

- [ ] Juice of 2 lemons
- [ ] Confectioners' sugar
- [ ] Your favorite fresh fruit—
    cantaloupes
    kiwi
    strawberries
    bananas
    oranges
    grapes

Sweetest Sweet Rolls

- [ ] 1 cup whole milk
- [ ] 6 tbsp. sugar
- [ ] 1 package active dry yeast
- [ ] 3¼ cups all-purpose flour
- [ ] 1 tsp. salt
- [ ] 1¼ cups unsalted butter
- [ ] 1 egg
- [ ] 1 tsp. vegetable oil
- [ ] ¾ cup light brown sugar
- [ ] 1 cup cornflakes
- [ ] 3 tbsp. ground cinnamon
- [ ] 2½ cups confectioners' sugar
- [ ] 4 tbsp. half and half
- [ ] 1 tsp. vanilla extract

Kettle Tea

- [ ] 1 cup milk
- [ ] 3 tsp. sugar
- [ ] ½ tsp. vanilla extract

Buffalo Chicken Wraps with Yummy Blue Cheese Dressing

- [ ] 6 boneless, skinless chicken breasts
- [ ] 2 tbsp. butter
- [ ] 6 tbsp. olive oil
- [ ] 4 tsp. Tabasco sauce
- [ ] 1 tsp. Creole seasoning
- [ ] 1 tsp. salt
- [ ] 1 tsp. pepper
- [ ] ¼ tsp. cayenne pepper
- [ ] ½ cup orange juice
- [ ] 1 tbsp. Dijon mustard
- [ ] 1 tsp. sugar
- [ ] 1½ cups celery
- [ ] 1½ cups carrots, shredded
- [ ] 2 cups cucumber
- [ ] ½ cup sour cream
- [ ] ¼ cup mayonnaise
- [ ] ½ cup blue cheese
- [ ] 1 tsp. cider vinegar
- [ ] 1 tsp. fresh lemon juice
- [ ] ½ tsp. onion
- [ ] Pinch garlic
- [ ] 12 soft flour tortillas

Of Course, Peanut Butter and Jelly Wraps

- [ ] ½ cup dried fruit bits
- [ ] ½ cup peanut butter
- [ ] ⅛ tsp. cinnamon
- [ ] ¼ cup your favorite jelly
- [ ] 6 soft flour tortillas

Lazy Morning Muffins

- [ ] 4½ cups flour
- [ ] 2½ cups sugar
- [ ] 2 tbsp. cinnamon
- [ ] 1 tsp. salt
- [ ] 4 tsp. baking soda
- [ ] 1 cup coconut
- [ ] ½ cup nuts (optional)
- [ ] 1 cup raisins
- [ ] 6 eggs
- [ ] 2¼ cups oil
- [ ] 2 tbsp. vanilla
- [ ] 2 cups mashed fruit (bananas, peaches, strawberries, apples)

Raw Veggies with Spicy Comeback Sauce

- ☐ Carrots
- ☐ Celery
- ☐ English cucumbers
- ☐ Black olives
- ☐ Cherry tomatoes
- ☐ 3 cloves garlic
- ☐ 1 medium onion
- ☐ ½ cup ketchup
- ☐ ½ cup chili sauce
- ☐ ½ cup oil
- ☐ 1 tbsp. paprika
- ☐ 1 tbsp. Worcestershire sauce
- ☐ 2 tbsp. fresh lemon juice
- ☐ 1 tsp. dry mustard
- ☐ 1½ tsp. Creole seasoning
- ☐ 1 cup mayonnaise

"Ice Chest" Strawberry Soup

- ☐ 5 cups strawberries
- ☐ ½ cup sugar
- ☐ 1 cup half and half
- ☐ 1 tsp. almond extract
- ☐ 1 cup sour cream

Mud 'N' Worms

- ☐ ¼ cup butter
- ☐ ½ cup sugar
- ☐ ¼ tsp. vanilla
- ☐ 1 large egg
- ☐ 1 cup all-purpose flour
- ☐ 3 tbsp. cocoa
- ☐ ⅛ tsp. salt
- ☐ Instant chocolate pudding mix (4-serving size)
- ☐ ½ cup sour cream
- ☐ 1 cup milk
- ☐ ½ cup chocolate cookie crumbs
- ☐ 24 gummy worms

Cheesy Meatloaf

- ☐ ¼ cup onion
- ☐ ½ cup celery
- ☐ 2 tsp. garlic
- ☐ 1 tsp. dried parsley
- ☐ 2 tsp. Creole seasoning
- ☐ ¼ tsp. pepper
- ☐ 1 tsp. chili powder
- ☐ 1 tsp. cumin
- ☐ ¾ cup salsa
- ☐ 3 eggs
- ☐ 1½ lb. lean ground beef or a mix of lean ground beef and ground turkey
- ☐ ¾ cup bread crumbs
- ☐ ½ lb. sliced mozzarella cheese

Carrot French Fries

- ☐ 2 lb. carrots
- ☐ 3 tbsp. butter
- ☐ 2 tsp. fresh rosemary (optional)
- ☐ ½ tsp. sugar
- ☐ ½ tsp. salt
- ☐ ¼ tsp. pepper

Creamed Corn

- ☐ 2 tbsp. butter
- ☐ ½ onion
- ☐ 3 tbsp. flour
- ☐ 1¾ cups milk
- ☐ 2½ cups corn, fresh (4 or 5 ears, cut off the cob)
- ☐ 1 tsp. sugar
- ☐ Salt and pepper

"Here's the Beef" Kebabs

- ☐ 2 cloves garlic
- ☐ 1 tbsp. sesame oil
- ☐ 1 tsp. honey
- ☐ 1 tbsp. lemon juice
- ☐ ½ cup soy sauce
- ☐ 1½ lb. London broil or round cut
- ☐ 1 large green pepper
- ☐ 1 large red pepper
- ☐ 5 small onions
- ☐ 10 fresh mushrooms
- ☐ 10 skewers
- ☐ 10 fresh rosemary sprigs or 2 tbsp. dried rosemary leaves

Broccoli Trees

- ☐ 1 lb. broccoli florets
- ☐ 4 tsp. Parmesan cheese, grated
- ☐ 2 tsp. lemon pepper

Volcano Potatoes

- ☐ 6 large potatoes
- ☐ 5 tbsp. butter
- ☐ 1 tsp. salt
- ☐ ¼ tsp. black pepper
- ☐ ⅓ cup milk
- ☐ 2 eggs
- ☐ 6 tbsp. cheddar cheese, grated

Golden Cheese Wedges

- ☐ 2 cups flour
- ☐ 1 tbsp. baking powder
- ☐ ¼ tsp. salt
- ☐ 5 tbsp. butter
- ☐ ⅔ cup milk
- ☐ ½ cup cheddar cheese, shredded

Tasty, Tender Pork Tenderloin

- ☐ 3 tbsp. soy sauce
- ☐ 3 tbsp. hoisin sauce
- ☐ 2 tbsp. oil
- ☐ 1½ tsp. sugar
- ☐ 1½ lb. pork tenderloin
- ☐ 2 tbsp. butter
- ☐ 1 quart Ziploc bag

Carrot Coins

- ☐ 10–12 medium-long, thin carrots
- ☐ 2 tbsp. butter
- ☐ ½ tsp. salt
- ☐ ¼ tsp. pepper
- ☐ 2 tsp. orange juice
- ☐ 2 tbsp. light brown sugar
- ☐ 2 tsp. sesame seeds

Creamy Dreamy Broccoli-Parmesan Risotto

- ☐ 6 cups chicken broth
- ☐ 1 onion
- ☐ 3 tbsp. olive oil
- ☐ 1½ cups rice, uncooked, short-grained (Arborio) or medium-grained rice
- ☐ 2 cups broccoli
- ☐ 1½ cups Parmesan cheese, grated
- ☐ ½ tsp. salt

Grandmother's Dinner Rolls

- ☐ 2 cups milk
- ☐ ½ cup sugar
- ☐ ½ cup vegetable shortening
- ☐ 1 package active dry yeast
- ☐ 4 cups all-purpose flour
- ☐ 1 tsp. baking soda
- ☐ 1 tsp. salt
- ☐ 1 tsp. baking powder

Dynamite Orange-Almond Salad

- [ ] ½ tsp. salt
- [ ] Pepper
- [ ] 2 tbsp. sugar
- [ ] 4 tbsp. vinegar
- [ ] ¼ cup oil
- [ ] 6 drops Tabasco sauce
- [ ] 2 tbsp. fresh parsley
- [ ] 1 15-oz can mandarin oranges
- [ ] ½ cup almonds, sliced
- [ ] 3 tbsp. sugar
- [ ] 1 bag mixed greens
- [ ] 2 green onions

Parmesan Cheese Biscuits

- [ ] 2 cups all-purpose flour
- [ ] ¼ tsp. baking soda
- [ ] 1 tbsp. baking powder
- [ ] 1 tsp. salt
- [ ] 6 tbsp. shortening
- [ ] ¾ cup buttermilk
- [ ] 1 cup Parmesan cheese, shredded

Hooray! for Hershey Bar Pie

- [ ] 6 Hershey bars with almonds
- [ ] ½ cup milk
- [ ] 20 large marshmallows
- [ ] 1 8-oz. carton Cool Whip
- [ ] 1 Chocolate Wafer Pie Crust

Chocolate Wafer Pie Crust

- [ ] 1 18-oz. package of Oreos or chocolate wafer cookies
- [ ] 6 tbsp. butter

Watermelon Cookies

- [ ] 3½ cups all-purpose flour
- [ ] 1½ tsp. baking powder
- [ ] 1 tsp. salt
- [ ] 1 cup butter
- [ ] 1½ cups sugar
- [ ] 1 tbsp. vanilla
- [ ] 2 eggs
- [ ] red and green food coloring
- [ ] 1 pkg. mini chocolate chips
- [ ] 2 cups powdered sugar

Myer's Favorite Buttermilk Pie

- [ ] 1 9-inch pie crust, or Homemade Pie Crust
- [ ] 1¼ cups sugar
- [ ] ½ cup butter
- [ ] 1 tbsp. flour
- [ ] 3 eggs
- [ ] ¾ cup buttermilk
- [ ] 1 tbsp. vanilla extract

Homemade Pie Crust

- [ ] 2 cups all-purpose flour
- [ ] 1 tsp. salt
- [ ] ⅔ cup shortening (for buttery flavor crust use butter-flavored shortening)

A⁺ Brownies

- [ ] 1 cup butter
- [ ] 4 1-oz. squares unsweetened chocolate
- [ ] 4 eggs
- [ ] 2 tsp. vanilla extract
- [ ] 2 cups sugar
- [ ] ½ tsp. salt
- [ ] ½ tsp. baking powder
- [ ] 1 cup flour
- [ ] 1 12-oz. package miniature chocolate chips

Everyone, Sit Down for Dinner

Wholesome Roasted Chicken
- [ ] 1 whole chicken (4–7 lb.)
- [ ] Olive oil
- [ ] Tabasco
- [ ] Salt
- [ ] Black pepper
- [ ] Lemon pepper
- [ ] Red pepper
- [ ] Paprika
- [ ] Garlic powder
- [ ] Season-All or any seasoned salt
- [ ] Rosemary

Sensational Succotash
- [ ] 1½ cups fresh or frozen corn kernels
- [ ] 1½ cups fresh or frozen lima beans

- [ ] 1 tbsp. butter
- [ ] ½ tsp. salt
- [ ] ¼ tsp. pepper
- [ ] ⅓ cup half and half

Martin's Baked Sweet Potatoes
- [ ] 6 large sweet potatoes
- [ ] 4 tbsp. unsalted butter
- [ ] 2 tsp. kosher salt

Cornbread Gems
- [ ] ½ cup yellow cornmeal
- [ ] 1 cup all-purpose flour
- [ ] 3 tsp. baking powder
- [ ] 2 tbsp. sugar
- [ ] 1 tsp. salt
- [ ] ¾ cup milk
- [ ] 1 egg
- [ ] 2 tbsp. butter

It's Italian!

Homemade Pasta Dough
- [ ] 3 cups white bread flour
- [ ] 4 large eggs
- [ ] 1 tsp. salt
- [ ] 1 tbsp. olive oil

Unrivaled Red Sauce
- [ ] 2 tbsp. olive oil
- [ ] 1½ cups yellow onion
- [ ] 2 tsp. garlic (4 cloves)
- [ ] ½ tsp. salt
- [ ] 2 tsp. Italian seasoning
- [ ] ¼ tsp. ground black pepper
- [ ] 1 28-oz. can tomato puree
- [ ] 2 15-oz. cans tomato sauce
- [ ] 1 6-oz. can tomato paste
- [ ] 1 tsp. sugar

Mighty Meatballs
- [ ] 2 large eggs

- [ ] ½ cup yellow onion
- [ ] 1½ lb. lean ground turkey or lean ground beef
- [ ] 1 tsp. garlic
- [ ] 2 tsp. Italian seasoning
- [ ] ½ tsp. ground black pepper
- [ ] 2 tsp. yellow mustard
- [ ] 2 tsp. ketchup
- [ ] ½ tsp. salt
- [ ] ½ tsp. Creole seasoning
- [ ] ½ cup Italian bread crumbs
- [ ] Flour
- [ ] 2 tbsp. of olive oil

Caesar Salad with Homemade Croutons
- [ ] 1¼ cups olive oil
- [ ] 1 cup Parmesan cheese, freshly grated
- [ ] 3 tbsp. garlic
- [ ] 1 tsp. fresh oregano

(continued on back)

South of the Border

Sour Cream Eat Ya Enchiladas
- [ ] 6 boneless, skinless chicken breasts
- [ ] Extra-virgin olive oil
- [ ] Creole seasoning
- [ ] 2 tbsp. butter
- [ ] 4 tbsp. onion
- [ ] 1 4.5-oz. can chopped green chiles
- [ ] 8 oz. cream cheese
- [ ] 8 oz. sour cream
- [ ] 1 12-count pkg. flour tortillas
- [ ] 12 oz. cheddar cheese, grated
- [ ] 12 oz. pepper jack cheese, grated
- [ ] 1 cup salsa

Fiesta Rice
- [ ] 4 tbsp. olive oil
- [ ] 1 large onion

- [ ] 1½ cups medium-grained rice
- [ ] 2 cloves garlic, or 1 tsp. garlic powder
- [ ] 2 8-oz. cans tomato sauce
- [ ] 1 tbsp. chili powder
- [ ] 1 tsp. salt
- [ ] ½ tsp. pepper
- [ ] 1 cup cheddar cheese, grated
- [ ] 2 cups Monterey Jack cheese, grated

Tempting Taco Quesadillas
- [ ] 1 lb. ground beef
- [ ] 1 package taco seasoning
- [ ] 2 avocados
- [ ] 8 oz. cheddar cheese, shredded
- [ ] 1 package soft flour tortillas
- [ ] Taco sauce

Unfancy French

Bistro Brown Sugar-Glazed Brie
- [ ] 1 lb. wheel of brie
- [ ] 1 cup pecans, chopped (optional)
- [ ] 2 cups light brown sugar
- [ ] ¼ cup butter
- [ ] crackers

Chicken & Mushroom Crêpes
- [ ] 12 Crêpes!!!
- [ ] 5 oz. fresh mushrooms
- [ ] 3 tbsp. butter
- [ ] ⅓ cup flour
- [ ] ¾ cup heavy cream
- [ ] ⅓ cup dry cooking sherry
- [ ] 4 oz. white cheddar cheese, grated
- [ ] 1 lb. chicken, cooked
- [ ] 1¼ cups chicken broth
- [ ] 4 tbsp. Parmesan cheese, grated

Crêpes!!!
- [ ] 3 large eggs
- [ ] 1½ cups milk
- [ ] 1¼ cup all-purpose flour
- [ ] 1 tbsp. sugar
- [ ] 2 tbsp. butter

Freshest French Green Beans (Haricot Verts)
- [ ] 1 lb. fresh green beans
- [ ] 1 tsp. salt
- [ ] 1 tbsp. butter
- [ ] Salt and Pepper
- [ ] ¼ cup heavy cream

Mixed Baby Greens with Fabulous French Dressing
- [ ] 2 12-oz. bags mixed baby salad greens
- [ ] 1 cup walnuts, chopped
- [ ] ½ cup red onion
- [ ] 1 avocado

(continued on back)

- [ ] 1 tsp. fresh thyme
- [ ] 1 pound day-old bread, preferably sourdough
- [ ] 1 egg
- [ ] 4 tbsp. fresh lemon juice
- [ ] 1 tsp. Worcestershire sauce
- [ ] ¼ tsp. red pepper flakes
- [ ] 1 tbsp. Dijon mustard
- [ ] 2 tsp. anchovy paste
- [ ] ¾ cup peanut oil
- [ ] Kosher salt and freshly ground black pepper
- [ ] 3 heads baby romaine lettuce, or 1 large head romaine lettuce

Crusty Italian Bread
- [ ] 1 pkg. rapid-rise dry yeast
- [ ] 1 tbsp. sugar
- [ ] 2½ cups bread flour
- [ ] 2½ tsp. salt
- [ ] 1 tsp. balsamic vinegar

- [ ] ¼ cup extra-virgin olive oil
- [ ] 2 tbsp. cornmeal

Favorite Fettuccine Alfredo
- [ ] 1 tbsp. salt
- [ ] 1 pound fettuccine pasta
- [ ] 2 cups heavy cream
- [ ] 2-3 cups Parmesan cheese, grated
- [ ] Salt and pepper
- [ ] Pinch of ground nutmeg

Totally Terrific Tiramisu
- [ ] 2 oz. dark chocolate
- [ ] 1 cup mascarpone cheese
- [ ] 8 oz. cream cheese
- [ ] 2 cups sour cream
- [ ] ½ cup sugar
- [ ] 1½ cups brewed decaf coffee (regular works too!)
- [ ] 20 lady fingers

Heavenly Butterfinger Dessert
- [ ] 16 oz. angel food cake
- [ ] 6 Butterfinger candy bars
- [ ] 1 pint whipping cream
- [ ] ¼ cup butter
- [ ] 2 eggs
- [ ] 2 tsp. vanilla extract
- [ ] 2 cups powdered sugar

Fabulous French Dressing
- [ ] 8 oz. garlic vinegar
- [ ] 2 tsp. salt
- [ ] 1 tsp. Tabasco sauce
- [ ] ⅛ tsp. red pepper
- [ ] 1 tsp. garlic powder
- [ ] ¼ tsp. paprika
- [ ] 3 heaping tsp. Dijon mustard
- [ ] 16 oz. (½ liter) olive oil

Paris Popovers
- [ ] 3 cups milk
- [ ] 3¾ cups all-purpose flour
- [ ] 1½ tsp. salt
- [ ] 1 tsp. baking powder
- [ ] 6 large eggs

Your Very Own Chocolate Soufflé with Vanilla Ice Cream
- [ ] ¼ cup butter
- [ ] ½ cup sugar
- [ ] 1 cup semisweet chocolate chips
- [ ] 3 tbsp. heavy cream
- [ ] 1 tbsp. flour
- [ ] 1 tbsp. vanilla extract
- [ ] 8 eggs
- [ ] 2 scoops vanilla ice cream

Mostly Mango Salsa
- [ ] 2 large mangoes
- [ ] 8 tomatillos
- [ ] 1 orange or yellow bell pepper
- [ ] ½ cup cilantro
- [ ] ½ cup red onion
- [ ] ¼ tsp. salt
- [ ] 1 tsp. ground cumin
- [ ] Juice from 1 lime

Nothing-to-It Nacho Breadsticks
- [ ] ¾ cup spicy nacho chips
- [ ] 1 11-oz. can refrigerated breadsticks

Mexican Made-in-the-Pan Chocolate Cake
- [ ] 1¼ cups all-purpose flour
- [ ] ⅓ cup unsweetened cocoa
- [ ] 1 cup sugar
- [ ] ½ tsp. salt
- [ ] ¾ tsp. baking soda
- [ ] ½ tsp. cinnamon
- [ ] ⅓ cup canola or vegetable oil
- [ ] 1 tsp. vanilla extract
- [ ] 1 tsp. cider or white vinegar

It's Greek to Me

Big Fat Greek Pizza
- [ ] 1 pkg. phyllo pastry dough
- [ ] ½ cup butter
- [ ] ½ cup olive oil
- [ ] 1 cup onions
- [ ] ¼ tsp. salt
- [ ] 3 large cloves garlic
- [ ] ½ tsp. dried basil
- [ ] ½ tsp. dried oregano
- [ ] Juice from ½ large lemon
- [ ] 1 pound fresh spinach, or 1 10-oz. pkg. frozen, chopped spinach
- [ ] 1 pound mozzarella cheese, grated
- [ ] 1½ cups crumbled feta or farmer's cheese
- [ ] 4 roma tomatoes
- [ ] ¾ cup fine bread crumbs
- [ ] Freshly ground black pepper

Feta Pita Toast
- [ ] 2 tbsp. butter
- [ ] ½ cup onion
- [ ] 8 oz. feta cheese
- [ ] ½ tsp. Greek seasoning
- [ ] Pinch cayenne pepper
- [ ] 1 pkg. pita bread
- [ ] ½ cup Parmesan cheese, grated

Pastitsio with Pizzazz!
- [ ] 1 tbsp. olive oil
- [ ] 1 medium onion
- [ ] 2 garlic cloves
- [ ] 1 pound lean ground beef
- [ ] 2 14.5-oz. cans diced tomatoes
- [ ] 2 tsp. dried oregano
- [ ] 1½ tsp. cinnamon
- [ ] 1¾ tsp. salt
- [ ] ¼ tsp. freshly ground pepper
- [ ] 8 oz. elbow macaroni
- [ ] 3 tbsp. butter
- [ ] ⅓ cup all-purpose flour
- [ ] 1 quart whole milk

(continued on back)

Sleepover Party

Creatures in a Blanket
- [ ] 2 8-oz. cans crescent dinner rolls
- [ ] 8 1-oz. slices cooked ham or turkey
- [ ] 8 single slices Swiss or cheddar cheese
- [ ] 16 frozen breaded wing-shaped chicken patties
- [ ] Squirt bottles of red ketchup, green or blue ketchup, and mustard

Pajama Peanut Butter Balls
- [ ] 1 cup peanut butter, creamy or crunchy
- [ ] 1 cup light corn syrup
- [ ] 1¼ cups powdered milk
- [ ] 1½ cups powdered sugar

All-Night Nacho Dip
- [ ] 2 8-oz. packages cream cheese
- [ ] 1 15-oz. can chili (no beans)
- [ ] 8 oz. Monterey Jack cheese, shredded, or a mixture of Monterey Jack and cheddar cheese
- [ ] Tortilla chips

No-Curfew Caramel Popcorn
- [ ] 1 cup sugar
- [ ] ½ cup butter
- [ ] ½ cup light corn syrup
- [ ] 1 tsp. salt
- [ ] 1 tsp. vanilla extract
- [ ] ½ tsp. baking soda
- [ ] 2 3-oz. packages microwave popcorn

Backyard Burger Bash

Rob's Grilled Cheddar Burgers
- [ ] 2 lb. ground chuck (20 percent fat is ideal)
- [ ] 2 tbsp. dill pickle juice
- [ ] 2 tbsp. Montreal Steak Seasoning
- [ ] 8 hamburger buns
- [ ] 8 slices cheddar cheese

Katie's Homemade Potato Chips
- [ ] 4 medium potatoes

Paint Magic
- [ ] ½ cup olive oil
- [ ] ¼ cup fresh lemon juice
- [ ] ¼ cup Worcestershire sauce
- [ ] 5 garlic cloves
- [ ] ½ tsp. black pepper

Slow-Cooked BBQ Baked Beans
- [ ] ¼ lb. bacon strips
- [ ] 1 medium onion
- [ ] 3 14.5-oz. cans pork and beans
- [ ] ½ cup ketchup
- [ ] 1 cup light brown sugar
- [ ] 2 tbsp. prepared mustard
- [ ] 2 tbsp. Worcestershire sauce
- [ ] 3 shakes Tabasco sauce

Pool Party

Annie's Sassy Salsa
- [ ] 2 15-oz. cans black beans
- [ ] 1 16-oz. can white corn
- [ ] ½ cup cilantro
- [ ] ¼ cup green onions
- [ ] ⅓ cup fresh lime juice
- [ ] 3 tbsp. olive oil
- [ ] 1 tbsp. cumin
- [ ] ½–1 tsp. salt
- [ ] Ground black pepper
- [ ] 1 4-oz. can chopped green chilies
- [ ] 4 dashes hot sauce

Baked Chicken Nuggets on a Stick
- [ ] 6 chicken breasts, boned and skinned
- [ ] ½ cup plain bread crumbs
- [ ] ¼ cup Parmesan cheese, grated
- [ ] 1 tsp. garlic salt
- [ ] ½ cup butter
- [ ] wooden skewers

Oven-Baked Corn-Dog Skewers
- [ ] 3 tbsp. yellow cornmeal
- [ ] 1 11.5-oz. can refrigerated cornbread twists or breadsticks
- [ ] 1 tbsp. prepared mustard
- [ ] 8 hotdogs
- [ ] wooden skewers

Didn't-Sleep-a-Wink Pink Drink

- ☐ 2 cups low-fat frozen vanilla yogurt
- ☐ 1 cup frozen sweetened strawberries
- ☐ 2 cups low-fat milk
- ☐ 8 cherries

- ☐ 2 large eggs
- ☐ 1 cup Parmesan cheese, crumbled
- ☐ 1 cup feta cheese

Mom's Marvelous Chicken Phyllo

- ☐ 6 cups cooked chicken breast
- ☐ 8 oz. cream cheese
- ☐ 1 bunch green onions
- ☐ 1 cup celery
- ☐ Salt and pepper
- ☐ 1 tsp. seafood seasoning
- ☐ ¼ cup dry cooking sherry
- ☐ 1 pkg. phyllo pastry dough
- ☐ 1¼ cup butter
- ☐ ¾ cup flour
- ☐ 1½ cups milk
- ☐ 1½ cups chicken broth

Tossed Greek Salad Bowl

- ☐ 1 head romaine lettuce
- ☐ ½ head iceberg lettuce

- ☐ 12 cherry tomatoes
- ☐ 1 cup feta, crumbled
- ☐ ½ small red onion
- ☐ 1 cucumber
- ☐ 12 kalamata olives
- ☐ 6 pepperoncini peppers
- ☐ 6 tbsp. olive oil
- ☐ 4 tbsp. fresh lemon juice
- ☐ 2 tsp. garlic
- ☐ 1 tsp. dried oregano
- ☐ 1 2-oz. can anchovies
- ☐ ½ tsp. salt
- ☐ ½ tsp. pepper
- ☐ ½ tsp. sugar

The Very Best Baklava

- ☐ 1 pkg. phyllo pastry
- ☐ ¾ cup butter
- ☐ ¾ cup light brown sugar
- ☐ ½ tsp. cinnamon
- ☐ ¼ tsp. allspice
- ☐ 2 cups pecans or walnuts, finely chopped

Poolside Potato Salad

- ☐ 2 pounds red new potatoes
- ☐ 2 tbsp. white vinegar
- ☐ 1 cup celery
- ☐ ½ cup onion
- ☐ ¼ cup fresh parsley
- ☐ 4 hard-boiled eggs
- ☐ 1 tsp. salt
- ☐ ¼ tsp. pepper
- ☐ ½ tsp. Creole seasoning
- ☐ 1½ cups mayonnaise
- ☐ 8 bacon slices

Summer Fruit Skewers

- ☐ strawberries
- ☐ apple wedges
- ☐ grapes
- ☐ melon
- ☐ pineapple
- ☐ oranges
- ☐ kiwi chunks
- ☐ straws

Caramel Fruit Dip

- ☐ ¼ cup sugar
- ☐ ¾ cup light brown sugar
- ☐ 1 tsp. vanilla extract
- ☐ 8 oz. cream cheese
- ☐ fresh fruit for dipping

Orange-Cream Fruit Dip

- ☐ 8 oz. cream cheese
- ☐ 7 oz. marshmallow crème
- ☐ 2 tbsp. fresh orange juice
- ☐ fresh fruit for dipping

On- or Off-the-Grill Buttered Corn

- ☐ 8 ears corn
- ☐ ½ cup butter
- ☐ 1 tsp. Creole seasoning
- ☐ 8 12- by 8-inch squares of aluminum foil

Backyard Brown Sugar Brownies

- ☐ 2 oz. unsweetened chocolate
- ☐ 1 cup all-purpose flour
- ☐ ½ tsp. salt
- ☐ 1 tsp. cinnamon
- ☐ ½ tsp. baking soda
- ☐ 1 cup butter
- ☐ 1¼ cups light brown sugar
- ☐ 1 large egg
- ☐ 1½ tsp. vanilla
- ☐ ⅓ cup sour cream
- ☐ 1 cup pecans (optional)
- ☐ 1½ cups powdered sugar
- ☐ 1 tbsp. milk

The Perfect Peach Blueberry Cobbler

- ☐ 4–5 large peaches
- ☐ 8 tbsp. unsalted butter
- ☐ 1 tbsp. lemon juice
- ☐ 1 cup sugar
- ☐ 1 cup fresh blueberries
- ☐ 1 cup all-purpose flour
- ☐ ½ tsp. salt
- ☐ 1½ tsp. baking powder
- ☐ 1 cup heavy cream
- ☐ 1 egg
- ☐ Vanilla ice cream

Re Re's Sand Cookies

- ☐ 1½ cups sugar
- ☐ ½ cup butter
- ☐ ½ cup shortening
- ☐ 1 egg
- ☐ 2½ cups flour
- ☐ ¾ tsp. salt
- ☐ ½ tsp. baking soda
- ☐ ½ tsp. baking powder
- ☐ 1 tsp. vanilla extract
- ☐ ½ tsp. almond extract
- ☐ 2 tbsp. milk

Christina's Scrumptious Bread Pudding with Fresh Berries

- ☐ 1 circular loaf of Hawaiian bread (1-pound loaf in tin)
- ☐ 3 cups heavy cream
- ☐ 1 cup milk
- ☐ 2½ tsp. vanilla extract
- ☐ 12 oz. white chocolate
- ☐ 7 eggs
- ☐ ¾ cup sugar
- ☐ 2 pinches salt
- ☐ Butter to coat pan
- ☐ 1 tsp. brandy (optional)
- ☐ 1 pound frozen raspberries or mixed berries
- ☐ Juice of half a lemon

Fresh berries:
- ☐ blueberries
- ☐ raspberries
- ☐ blackberries
- ☐ strawberries

Perfect Pizza Crust

- ☐ 1 pkg. active dry yeast
- ☐ 1 tbsp. honey
- ☐ 3 tbsp. extra-virgin olive oil
- ☐ 1 tsp. salt
- ☐ 3½ cups all-purpose flour
- ☐ ½ cup bread flour

Best BBQ Chicken Pizza!

- ☐ 2 lb. chicken
- ☐ ½ cup barbecue sauce
- ☐ 1½ tsp. olive oil
- ☐ 1 cup mozzarella cheese, shredded
- ☐ ½ cup smoked Gouda cheese, grated
- ☐ ½ cup red onion
- ☐ 2 tsp. fresh cilantro
- ☐ Pizza crust

It-Only-Takes-a-Minute Pizza

- ☐ 1 16.3-oz. can refrigerated big biscuits

Choice of toppings:
- ☐ pepperoni
- ☐ Canadian bacon
- ☐ mushrooms
- ☐ black olives
- ☐ 1 cup of pizza sauce
- ☐ 1½ cups mozzarella cheese, grated

Everyone Loves Cookie Pizza!

Pizza Crust:
- ☐ 2 eggs
- ☐ 1 cup light brown sugar
- ☐ ½ cup sugar
- ☐ 1 cup butter
- ☐ 2 tsp. vanilla
- ☐ 2½ cup flour
- ☐ 1 tsp. baking soda

Chocolate Pizza Sauce:
- ☐ 3 cups confectioners' sugar
- ☐ 3 tbsp. cocoa powder
- ☐ 4 tbsp. milk
- ☐ 4 tbsp. butter
- ☐ 1 tsp. vanilla extract
- ☐ Pinch salt

Toppings:
Choose from these topping ideas:
- ☐ multicolored sprinkles
- ☐ colored sugar
- ☐ mini chocolate chips
- ☐ gummy worms
- ☐ silver balls
- ☐ mini-marshmallows
- ☐ M&Ms

All American Green Apple Pizza

- ☐ 2½ cups all-purpose flour
- ☐ 2 cups quick-cooking rolled oats
- ☐ 1½ cups light brown sugar
- ☐ 1 tsp. baking soda
- ☐ 1¼ cups margarine or butter
- ☐ 1½ cups caramel ice cream topping
- ☐ 2 cups Granny Smith apples

Phillip's Cheese Soup

- ☐ 4 tbsp. butter
- ☐ ½ cup carrots
- ☐ ½ cup green pepper
- ☐ ½ cup onion
- ☐ ½ cup celery
- ☐ ½ cup flour
- ☐ 3 cans chicken broth
- ☐ 12 oz. medium cheddar cheese, grated
- ☐ 4 cups milk
- ☐ Salt and white pepper

Hearty Chili

- ☐ 1 28-oz. can crushed tomatoes
- ☐ 1 can Rotel tomatoes
- ☐ 3 lb. coarsely ground lean beef
- ☐ 1 large onion
- ☐ 2 cloves garlic
- ☐ 2 bay leaves
- ☐ 1 tsp. oregano
- ☐ 2 tsp. ground cumin
- ☐ 1 tsp. salt
- ☐ 3 tbsp. chili powder
- ☐ 2 tsp. black pepper
- ☐ 1 tbsp. Southwest seasoning
- ☐ 2 tbsp. fresh cilantro
- ☐ 3 tbsp. flour

Flavorful Tortilla Soup

- ☐ 6 chicken breasts
- ☐ 2 onions
- ☐ 2 bay leaves
- ☐ 1 tsp. salt
- ☐ 1 tsp. pepper
- ☐ 4 cloves garlic
- ☐ 3 ribs celery
- ☐ 1 green pepper
- ☐ 1 jalapeno
- ☐ 2 tbsp. olive oil
- ☐ 1 can tomato soup
- ☐ 1 can Rotel tomatoes
- ☐ 1 tsp. cumin
- ☐ 2 tsp. chili powder
- ☐ ½ tsp. salt
- ☐ ½ tsp. pepper

(continued on back)

Design Your Own! Pizza

- [ ] 1 refrigerated canned pizza crust
- [ ] Pizza sauce

Choice of toppings:
- [ ] pepperoni
- [ ] Canadian bacon
- [ ] broccoli
- [ ] bacon
- [ ] hamburger meat
- [ ] mushrooms
- [ ] fresh basil
- [ ] roasted red peppers
- [ ] Parmesan cheese
- [ ] mozzarella cheese
- [ ] cheddar cheese
- [ ] black olives

Farm Fresh Pizza

Crust:
- [ ] 2 cups all-purpose flour
- [ ] 1½ tsp. baking powder
- [ ] 1 tsp. sugar
- [ ] ½ tsp. salt
- [ ] ¼ cup butter
- [ ] ¾ cup cheddar cheese, grated
- [ ] ¾ cup milk

Toppings:
- [ ] 1 tbsp. butter
- [ ] 8 large eggs
- [ ] Salt and pepper
- [ ] 1 16-oz. tube sausage, or 1 lb. bacon
- [ ] 1½ cups cheddar cheese, grated

- [ ] 1 tbsp. Worcestershire sauce
- [ ] 3 corn tortillas

For garnishing:
- [ ] Cheddar cheese, grated
- [ ] Monterey Jack cheese, grated
- [ ] Sour cream

Cozy Cream of Tomato Soup

- [ ] 3 tbsp. olive oil
- [ ] 1 large onion
- [ ] 1 28-oz. can crushed tomatoes
- [ ] 2 cups tomato juice
- [ ] ½ tsp. salt
- [ ] ¼ tsp. pepper
- [ ] 1 cup heavy cream

Roll-Over-and-Play-Sick Soup

- [ ] 2 lb. round steak
- [ ] 1 tbsp. olive oil
- [ ] 2 medium onions
- [ ] 1½ cups celery
- [ ] 6 medium carrots
- [ ] 1 10-oz. pkg. frozen sliced okra

- [ ] 1 10-oz. pkg. frozen baby lima beans
- [ ] 1 10-oz. pkg. frozen corn
- [ ] 3 14.5-oz. cans beef broth
- [ ] 2 cans Rotel tomatoes
- [ ] 2 bay leaves
- [ ] 1 tsp. salt
- [ ] 1 tsp. pepper
- [ ] 2 tsp. spicy spaghetti seasoning (or Italian seasoning)
- [ ] 1 tsp. Creole seasoning
- [ ] 1 tbsp. soy sauce

Simple Shrimp Chowder

- [ ] 1 tbsp. butter
- [ ] 1 onion
- [ ] 2 10¾-oz. cans cream of potato soup
- [ ] 3¼ cups milk
- [ ] ½ tsp. liquid crab boil
- [ ] ¼ tsp. ground pepper
- [ ] ⅛ tsp. salt
- [ ] 1½ lb. medium-sized fresh or frozen shrimp
- [ ] 1 cup Monterey Jack cheese, shredded

Keep Your Eyes on Pies

Comfy Chicken Pot Pie

- [ ] 2 pie crusts
- [ ] ⅓ cup margarine or butter
- [ ] ⅓ cup onion
- [ ] ⅓ cup all-purpose flour
- [ ] ½ tsp. salt
- [ ] ¼ tsp. pepper
- [ ] ¼ tsp. Creole seasoning
- [ ] 1 14-oz. can chicken broth
- [ ] ⅓ cup milk
- [ ] 2½ cups cooked chicken
- [ ] 1¾ cups frozen mixed vegetables

Susie Shepherd's Pie

- [ ] 6 cups potatoes
- [ ] 2 tsp. salt, plus salt to taste
- [ ] 4 tbsp. butter
- [ ] 1 cup sour cream
- [ ] ¼ cup milk
- [ ] 2 lb. ground beef

- [ ] ½ cup flour
- [ ] 1 tbsp. Creole seasoning
- [ ] 1 tbsp. Italian seasoning
- [ ] ¼ tsp. pepper
- [ ] ¾ cup onions
- [ ] ½ cup green onions
- [ ] 3 tbsp. garlic
- [ ] 1½ cups beef broth
- [ ] 1½-2 cups cheddar cheese, grated
- [ ] Fresh parsley
- [ ] Paprika

Favorite Sloppy Joe Pie

- [ ] 1½ lb. lean ground beef
- [ ] ½ cup green onions
- [ ] 1 15.5-oz. can Sloppy Joe sauce
- [ ] 1 11-oz. can Mexican whole kernel corn
- [ ] 1 6-oz. can refrigerated buttermilk flaky biscuits

Keep Your Eyes on Pies (cont.)

Tastiest Toffee Ice Cream Pie

Toffee Ice Cream Pie:

- [ ] 1 Chocolate Wafer Crust
- [ ] 6 oz. chocolate toffee candy bars (Heath Bars)
- [ ] 1 pint vanilla ice cream

Chocolate Silk Sauce:

- [ ] ¼ cup butter
- [ ] 1 cup milk chocolate chips
- [ ] 1¼ cups powdered sugar
- [ ] 1 5½-oz. can evaporated milk
- [ ] 1 tsp. vanilla extract

Old-Fashioned Pecan Pie

- [ ] 1 Homemade Pie Crust
- [ ] ½ cup light brown sugar
- [ ] ½ cup sugar
- [ ] 3 tbsp. flour
- [ ] 1 cup light corn syrup
- [ ] ½ tsp. vanilla extract

- [ ] ⅛ tsp. salt
- [ ] 3 eggs
- [ ] ¼ cup butter
- [ ] 1 cup pecan halves

Homemade Pie Crust

- [ ] 2 cups all-purpose flour
- [ ] 1 tsp. salt
- [ ] ⅔ cup shortening (for buttery flavor crust use butter-flavored shortening)

Delightful Cheese Pie

- [ ] 1 9-in. Graham Cracker Pie Crust
- [ ] 2 8-oz. pkg. cream cheese
- [ ] 2 eggs
- [ ] 1¼ cup sugar
- [ ] 4 tsp. vanilla
- [ ] Juice of one lemon (1 tbsp.)
- [ ] 8 oz. sour cream

Bake Sale Favorites

Glazed Sugar Cookies

- [ ] 1 cup butter
- [ ] 1½ cups sugar
- [ ] 2 tsp. cream of tartar
- [ ] 1 tsp. baking soda
- [ ] ¼ tsp. salt
- [ ] 2 eggs
- [ ] 2 tsp. vanilla extract
- [ ] 2½ cups all-purpose flour
- [ ] 3-4 tsp. milk
- [ ] ½ tsp. almond extract
- [ ] Assorted food color
- [ ] 1 cup confectioners' sugar
- [ ] Sprinkles, optional

Leslie's Fluffy Ladies

- [ ] 1 roll refrigerated chocolate chip cookie dough
- [ ] 6 oz. semisweet choc. chips
- [ ] 1 12-oz. bag caramels
- [ ] 3 tbsp. half and half
- [ ] 1 cup pecans, chopped

Poppy Seed Bread

- [ ] 2 cups sugar
- [ ] 1¼ cup oil

- [ ] 4 eggs
- [ ] 1 12-oz. can evaporated milk
- [ ] 4 cups all-purpose flour
- [ ] 4 tsp. baking powder
- [ ] 1 tsp. salt
- [ ] 1 tsp. vanilla
- [ ] ½ cup poppy seeds

Conglomerations

- [ ] 1 cup butter
- [ ] 1 lb. confectioners' sugar
- [ ] 1½ cups crunchy or creamy peanut butter
- [ ] 12 graham crackers
- [ ] 6 1.55-oz. Hershey milk chocolate bars

La-Te-Dahs!

- [ ] 2 cups unsalted butter
- [ ] 1 cup dark brown sugar
- [ ] 1 cup light brown sugar
- [ ] 3 large eggs
- [ ] 1 tbsp. vanilla
- [ ] 2 tbsp. cinnamon
- [ ] ½ tsp. ginger

(continued on back)

Bake Sale Favorites (cont.)

Granny's Cheese Straws

- [ ] 1 cup margarine
- [ ] 12 oz. extra sharp cheddar cheese, grated
- [ ] 2 cups flour
- [ ] ⅛ tsp. salt
- [ ] ½ tsp. cayenne or red pepper

Royal Carrot Cake

- [ ] 3½ cups sugar
- [ ] 2¼ cup flour
- [ ] 1¾ tsp. salt
- [ ] 1½ cups heavy cream
- [ ] 1¾ cup butter
- [ ] 2¼ cups pecans, chopped
- [ ] 3 tbsp. vanilla extract
- [ ] 1¼ cups corn oil
- [ ] 2 tsp. cinnamon
- [ ] 2 tsp. baking powder
- [ ] 1 tsp. baking soda
- [ ] 4 eggs
- [ ] 4 cups carrots, grated
- [ ] 1 cup raisins
- [ ] 8 oz. cream cheese

- [ ] 1 1-lb. box powdered sugar
- [ ] 1½ cups sweetened shredded coconut

Gingersnaps

- [ ] ¾ cup butter
- [ ] 1½ cup sugar
- [ ] ¼ cup molasses
- [ ] ¼ tsp. salt
- [ ] 1 tsp. cinnamon
- [ ] 2 tsp. baking soda
- [ ] 1 tsp. cloves
- [ ] 1 tsp. ginger
- [ ] 2 cups all-purpose flour

Tunnel of Fudge Cake

- [ ] 1¾ cups butter
- [ ] 1¾ cups sugar
- [ ] 6 eggs
- [ ] 2¾ cups powdered sugar
- [ ] 2¼ cups all-purpose flour
- [ ] 1 cup cocoa
- [ ] 2 cups walnuts, chopped
- [ ] 3½-4 tbsp. milk

Sweetheart Fudge Pie

- ☐ ½ cup butter
- ☐ ¾ cup light brown sugar
- ☐ 3 eggs
- ☐ 1 12-oz. pkg. semisweet chocolate chips
- ☐ 1 tsp. instant coffee
- ☐ 1 tsp. vanilla
- ☐ ½ cup all-purpose flour
- ☐ 1 cup walnuts or pecans, chopped
- ☐ 1 9-in. Cream Cheese Pie Crust

Cream Cheese Pie Crust

- ☐ 1 cup all-purpose flour
- ☐ ¼ cup powdered sugar
- ☐ Pinch salt
- ☐ ½ cup unsalted butter
- ☐ 4 oz. cream cheese

Graham Cracker Pie Crust

- ☐ 2 cups finely ground graham crackers
- ☐ ½ cup unsalted butter

Chocolate Wafer Pie Crust

- ☐ 1 18-oz. pkg.Oreos or chocolate wafer cookies
- ☐ 6 tbsp. butter

William's Deep-Dish Pizza Pie

- ☐ 1 lb. lean ground beef
- ☐ ¾ cup onion
- ☐ 1 8-oz. jar pizza sauce
- ☐ 1 11-oz. can refrigerated crusty French loaf
- ☐ 1 cup mozzarella cheese, shredded
- ☐ 1 cup Parmesan cheese, shredded
- ☐ 1 3-oz. pkg. sliced pepperoni
- ☐ 1 egg

Classic Chicken Spaghetti Pie

- ☐ 2 lb. boneless, skinless chicken breast
- ☐ 2 14-oz. cans cream of mushroom soup
- ☐ 1 bell pepper
- ☐ ½ cup celery
- ☐ 2 cloves garlic

- ☐ 2 onions
- ☐ 1 tbsp. butter
- ☐ 1 16-oz. pkg. spaghetti
- ☐ 1 egg
- ☐ ⅓ cup slivered almonds
- ☐ ⅓ cup cooking sherry
- ☐ 1 tbsp. Worcestershire sauce
- ☐ Salt and pepper
- ☐ 1 cup Parmesan cheese, shredded

My Oh My Apple Pie

- ☐ 5 cups apples
- ☐ 1½ cups light brown sugar
- ☐ 1 cup all-purpose flour
- ☐ ¾ cup butter
- ☐ 1½ tsp. cinnamon

Grandmother's No-Fail Pumpkin Bread

- ☐ 3 cups sugar
- ☐ 1 cup canola or vegetable oil
- ☐ 3 eggs
- ☐ 2 cups canned pumpkin
- ☐ 3 cups all-purpose flour
- ☐ ½ tsp. baking soda
- ☐ 1 tsp. salt
- ☐ 1 tsp. cinnamon
- ☐ 1 tsp. nutmeg

So Good Banana Bread

- ☐ ½ cup shortening
- ☐ ½ cup butter
- ☐ 2 cups sugar
- ☐ 1 cup light brown sugar
- ☐ 2 tsp. vanilla
- ☐ 4 eggs
- ☐ ½ tsp. salt
- ☐ 3½ cups all-purpose flour
- ☐ 2 tsp. baking soda
- ☐ ½ cup buttermilk
- ☐ 6 small bananas
- ☐ 1 cup pecans, chopped

Sterling's Simply Spectacular Brownies

- ☐ 1 cup butter
- ☐ 2½ cups sugar
- ☐ 2 squares unsweetened baking chocolate
- ☐ 1 square semisweet baking chocolate
- ☐ 2 pinches salt
- ☐ 1½ cups all-purpose flour
- ☐ ½ tsp. baking powder
- ☐ 4 eggs
- ☐ 2 tsp. vanilla extract

Kim's Raspberry Bars

- ☐ 2 cups all-purpose flour
- ☐ 2 cups light brown sugar
- ☐ ¾ cup butter
- ☐ 1¼ cup seedless raspberry preserves, or apricot preserves
- ☐ ⅛ tsp. salt
- ☐ 1 tsp. almond extract
- ☐ 1 cup powdered sugar
- ☐ 1 tbsp. milk

- ☐ 2 cups sugar
- ☐ 2 cups flour
- ☐ 2 tsp. salt
- ☐ 2 tsp. baking soda
- ☐ 3 cups quick-cooking oatmeal
- ☐ 2 cups walnut pieces
- ☐ 1 cup raisins

Rob's Ranger Cookies

- ☐ 1 cup butter-flavor shortening
- ☐ 1 cup sugar
- ☐ 1 cup light brown sugar
- ☐ 2 eggs
- ☐ 1 tsp. vanilla
- ☐ 2 cups all-purpose flour
- ☐ 1 tsp. baking soda
- ☐ 1 tsp. baking powder
- ☐ ½ tsp. salt
- ☐ 2 cups quick-cooking oatmeal
- ☐ 2 cups Rice Krispies

Mrs. Todd's Cream Cheese Pound Cake

- ☐ 3 cups sugar
- ☐ 1½ cups butter

- ☐ 8 oz. cream cheese
- ☐ 3 cups all-purpose flour
- ☐ ½ tsp. salt
- ☐ 6 eggs
- ☐ 1 tbsp. lemon extract
- ☐ 1 tbsp. almond extract

Helen's Peanut Butter M&M Cookies

- ☐ 2 cups flour
- ☐ 1 tsp. baking soda
- ☐ 1 tsp. salt
- ☐ ¼ tsp. cinnamon
- ☐ ¾ cup unsalted butter
- ☐ ¾ cup peanut butter
- ☐ 1 cup sugar
- ☐ 1 cup light brown sugar
- ☐ 2 eggs
- ☐ 1 tsp. vanilla extract
- ☐ ¼ cup milk
- ☐ 2 cups old fashioned oatmeal
- ☐ 12-oz. bag of M&M baking chips